# Birth
# Order

# Birth
# Order

### What your position in the family *really* tells you about your character

piatkus

PIATKUS

First published in Great Britain in 2011 by Piatkus

Copyright © 2011 by Linda Blair

The moral right of the author has been asserted.

A CIP catalogue record for this book
is available from the British Library.

ISBN 978-0-7499-4009-6

Typeset in ITC Stone Serif by Palimpsest Book Production Limited,
Falkirk, Stirlingshire

Printed and bound in Great Britain by the
MPG Books Group, Bodmin, Cornwall

Papers used by Piatkus are natural, renewable and recyclable
products sourced from well-managed forests and certified
in accordance with the rules of the Forest Stewardship Council.

**Mixed Sources**
Product group from well-managed
forests and other controlled sources
www.fsc.org  Cert no. SGS-COC-004081
© 1996 Forest Stewardship Council

FSC

Piatkus
An imprint of
Little, Brown Book Group
100 Victoria Embankment
London EC4Y 0DY

An Hachette UK Company
www.hachette.co.uk

www.piatkus.co.uk

To my brother and sisters,
Paul, Becca, Judy, Penny and Christen

# Acknowledgements

My deepest appreciation and thanks go to my patients who, during the thirty years I've been working as a clinical psychologist, have taught me so much about human nature and about how family members interact with and benefit from one another.

I also owe a big debt to my agents Amanda Preston and Luigi Bonomi, and to my editorial team at Piatkus – Jillian Stewart, Gill Bailey and Paola Ehrlich. When I was writing this book, I found it difficult to strike the right balance between academic findings, so that what I tell you has validity and reliability, and clinical anecdotes, so that what you read is realistic and engaging. At times I felt this was an impossible balance to achieve, and I probably would have given up the struggle if it hadn't been for the continual suggestions and encouragement I received from these professionals.

Finally, I wish to thank my family – my husband Rob and my children Jon, Sam and Katy, and Jon's wife Helen. No one ever complained about my frequent mental absences as I structured and restructured what I was trying to convey, and everyone helped out whenever they could (regardless of their birth order position), so I had the time to write. Thanks.

# Linda Blair

Born to parents who worked in the medical profession, Linda grew up in Kansas, the eldest of six children. At eighteen, she attended Wellesley College in Massachusetts, where she discovered her passion for psychology and literature. After graduating in psychology, she moved to England for three years. For part of this time she worked in the Medical Research Council's animal behaviour unit at Cambridge University, studying mother–infant relationships in primates with Professor Robert Hinde. This convinced her to learn more about developmental psychology, and she was awarded a scholarship at Harvard to study children's play and linguistic development. She returned to London in 1978 to begin her clinical training, qualifying as a clinical psychologist in 1980 after studying at the Maudsley Hospital. After learning German in Munich that summer, she returned to Cambridge to take up an NHS post working with the elderly.

Two years later she took up another NHS job, this time working with children and their families. She adopted her first son, Jonathan, during this period and switched from full-time to part-time work.

Over the next fifteen years, as her family size increased from one to three children, Linda worked in a number of part-time jobs for the NHS, the Medical Research Council and the University of Cambridge. She also started her own private practice as a clinical psychologist specialising in cognitive therapy and, in the late 1980s, began giving talks in schools and universities about how to cope with exam stress, both of which she continues with today.

In 2000, Linda moved with her husband and children to Bath, where she worked in the University of Bath Medical Centre offering cognitive therapy to students and staff. By the end of 2004, her writing and media work had become so time-consuming that she gave up her university position.

Linda's writing and media career began by chance, in Cambridge in the 1980s. The local BBC radio station asked the Cambridge psychology department if someone would be available to take part in a discussion about phobias. Linda was the only psychologist free at that time, and so she joined in. She was asked to return for a regular weekly programme, and now broadcasts frequently on Radios 4 and 2, BBC Radio Wales and the World Service. She has also appeared in a number of television shows including *Child of Our Time,* *Mindshock* (about children raised without human language), *Yesterday Once More* (the life of Karen Carpenter), *Kilroy* and the *Ruby Wax Show.* She's quoted regularly in newspapers and magazines, and has had columns in the *Guardian* and in *Psychologies* magazine. She now has a regular column in *The Times* and in *Junior* magazine. She's also a trustee for the charity Kidscape.

Linda is a member of the media committee which the British Psychological Society recommends to the press, television and radio commentators. Her professional qualifications include chartered status with the British Psychological Society (she is an Associate Fellow) and accreditation with the British Association for Behavioural and Cognitive Psychotherapies. She's also a Chartered Scientist. Her chief interests are her family, her dogs and cat, sport (particularly swimming, yoga and walking), cooking, gardening, literature and just about anything psychological.

# Contents

# Introduction

There's probably no subject that fascinates us as much as human character. We all want to get to know ourselves better and to feel as comfortable as possible with the way we think, feel and behave. Perhaps that's why the birth-order theory captures our imagination – it offers a tantalisingly simple means of understanding ourselves and others. But how much can it really tell you? Can it give you an understanding of how you've come to be the way you are? Can it help you to predict the way you'll behave in certain situations, and how you'll interact with other people?

Many of us sense – quite rightly, I think – that our place in the family must make a difference. Whether we were the first, the middle, the last or the only child must influence the way we think, feel and behave. So why, then, do so many of us end up feeling unsatisfied when we try to work out the precise role that birth order plays in character formation? Why do the descriptions never turn out to be an exact fit?

The reason, I believe, is that no one has looked at the *relative* role that birth-order plays – that is, whether it's sufficient on its own, or whether it's only one piece of the puzzle that's you. Although there are plenty of explanations of 'typical' birth order characteristics, I don't think birth order has itself ever been put into a proper context.

As anyone who's studied human nature carefully knows, a number of factors are constantly at work, helping to shape your character from the moment you first draw breath – how you were parented, whether you grew up in one place or moved repeatedly, whether your parents split up or stayed together, any traumatic events you've experienced and so on.

Of course, we all continue to develop to some extent throughout our lives, but the foundations of character are established in childhood, primarily in the early years, from conception until we're settled in school, around the age of six or seven. Experiences throughout later childhood and adolescence – even adulthood – matter, of course, but to a lesser extent. So I'll be focusing, in the main, on the early years, considering questions such as these:

- What makes each individual – even identical twins raised in the same home by the same parents – unique?

- Why are some people more ambitious than others?

- Why are some people self-confident while others are so unsure of themselves?

While a number of forces influence character and *could* be considered, I've singled out those that I believe exert the most powerful and long-lasting effects on us all. Effectively, I've navigated the minefield of potential influences on character to present you with the most likely candidates.

## How Can This Knowledge Benefit You?

### Get to know yourself better

Appraising the ways in which you fit in to your birth-order profile, as well as how you differ from it, is a powerful catalyst to get you thinking about the past – how you were parented, your relationships with siblings and others, shake-ups in your home life and so on. By going through this process you'll be able to see more clearly how you were influenced, and how and when you changed as you grew up.

What you'll learn here can also help you understand more clearly why you form the relationships you do now, and why some of them seem so comfortable and easy to maintain, while others are more problematic. You'll begin to see how, throughout your life, the relationships you seek reflect the patterns you formed in childhood.

## Understand the other people in your life

If you know a person's birth-order position, you'll already be able to guess a great deal about the way they behave, think and feel. By asking a few more questions about their background – based on the other important influences I outline – you'll be able to understand even more about their character and what motivates them.

## View life choices in a new light

Armed with so much new information about yourself and those around you, you will learn to think about people in richer and more complex ways than ever before – knowing that character is the result of a number of interweaving factors. Your new perspective on human nature will be invaluable in helping you to assess the best course of action when presented with important choices – be it the best choice of partner or whether or not to go down a particular career path.

## How to Use This Book

The book is divided into two parts. In Part One you will read about the four main birth-order positions – first, middle, last and single children – and the features that are the most typical for each of them. I'll also provide you with a snapshot of the standard family environment for each position from the point of view of someone in that particular place in the family constellation, and consider the best choice of partner and career for them. So Part One is the foundation that will help you to understand your character.

In Part Two, I fill out the birth-order picture and make those 'typical' characteristics you learned about in Part One more meaningful. Four main factors are considered in order to turn the standard list into something more personal and each of these has its own chapter:

- **Your parents** What were your primary carers like? (By 'primary carers' I mean whoever you considered to be your parent(s); this will probably be your biological parents, but it could be adopting parents, step-parents, guardians or grandparents.) What were their attitudes towards parenting in general and towards you in particular? How were they parented themselves when they were young? What was happening to them when you were growing up?

- **Your siblings** Here we consider the effects that the spacing between you and your siblings, the gender of each sibling and the total number of children in your family may have had on you when you were growing up. I also look at the powerful influence that the death of a sibling may have had or how a sibling with special needs may have affected your character.

- **Shake-ups in family structure** These are the events that cause a family to reorganise itself – parental separation and divorce, new partners and remarriage and the establishing of step-families – and their effects. We'll also examine the impact of moving house, the return of an older sibling who has moved away from the family home and the introduction of frail or infirm relatives.

- **Other key relationships** Did a relative, teacher, friend, friend's parents or someone else outside the family play an important role in your development and influence your beliefs or attitudes when you were growing up? We'll consider the ways in which these individuals can affect character. We'll also define 'abuse' and look at the possible consequences of such a relationship on your character.

In addition, I consider two other factors in your development. They are the relative roles of genetic and environmental influences on character, and something I refer to as 'flashbulb moments'. These have their part to play in the formation of your character and they'll interact with 'typical' birth-order characteristics too – although, perhaps, to a lesser extent than the four factors above.

Both Part One and Part Two can be read on their own. So you may decide that you'd simply like to learn about the traits that characterise a particular birth-order position and how this is likely to interact with your choice of partner and career – in which case you'll want to turn to Part One. If you wish to learn about the factors that influence and modify the 'typical' characteristics of each birth position, look at Part Two. This will enable you to shape and reorganise what's 'typical' into a more accurate picture of yourself. By putting both Parts One and Two together, you can create a revealing profile for yourself (or someone you wish to know more about) that will enrich your understanding of why you (or they) think, feel and behave the way you do.

I've included case studies throughout the book, which will help to make the knowledge I share with you more personal. I've been working as a cognitive therapist for over thirty years now, so I'm fortunate to have a great deal of material from which to choose. In a sense, therefore, you'll be learning not only from me, but also from the hundreds of people who've come to see me and shared their experiences so honestly and openly in my clinics. The case studies are all based on real clinical cases. However, names and details have been changed and cases have been amalgamated so that confidentiality is respected and individual privacy is protected.

## About Me

Because this book is all about how family circumstances and background can shape character, it's only natural that you might want to know a bit about me.

I grew up in the Midwest in America in the 1950s and '60s, the eldest of six closely spaced children – five girls and one boy. My parents both worked long hours. This was fairly unusual in those days and childcare was hard to find, so I was given a great deal of responsibility early on to care for my brother and sisters.

If I could define my parents' cardinal rule when parenting us, it would be that the only way to succeed is through sheer hard work. Furthermore, they believed that anyone can do just about anything if he or she simply tries hard enough and keeps at it for long enough. My parents expected us to set extremely high goals and standards for ourselves and then to work single-mindedly until we achieved them.

Because my parents were so preoccupied with their own careers, the six of us children were often left to fend for ourselves. Consequently, we came to rely on one another, probably more so than we did on any adults in our lives. As a result, my relationships with my brother and sisters were – and still are – some of the most important in my life.

We also had a very close relationship with our maternal grandparents, who, although they lived 700 miles away, often came to stay and look after us. I – more than any of my siblings, I think – regarded my grandparents as my main carers. I suspect that this was because my parents gave me greater responsibility than I wanted or felt ready to cope with, so I turned elsewhere to be looked after and nurtured myself.

I now have three children of my own. The elder two are boys and the youngest is a girl, and all three were adopted as babies. Because I knew very little about their backgrounds, I could only watch and guess what their biological parents might be like. I think the fact that it was impossible to hold many preconceptions about how they'd develop meant that each of them had a good chance to cultivate and display their own unique characteristics. They're certainly very different from one another in character, and they've chosen very different career paths.

As the mother of adopted children, I've also been particularly aware of the powerful influence of the position in the family that a child grows up in as opposed to their biological birth-order position: although each of my three was a first born in their biological family, they've grown up with the pressures and advantages typical for a first, a middle and a youngest child respectively. You can see in each of them many of the characteristics typical of their position in the family.

My eldest son likes to lead and to take responsibility. He's competitive and he sets extremely high goals for himself. My 'middle' son's characteristics are complicated by the fact that he has a disability, so in many ways he's not a typical middle born anyway. On the other hand, he's easily convinced by the opinions of others, he dresses unconventionally and he left school to pursue a non-academic training. My 'last born', as the youngest in our family, is extremely creative and loves to challenge established views. At the same time, however, as my only daughter, she's also a 'first born' (this is something you'll learn more about in Part Two) and has a number of first-born traits as well – she's organised and responsible, she sets herself high standards and she's done extremely well academically.

Of course, this is only the anecdotal evidence of one family, but I believe it does suggest what a strong effect birth-order position can have.

## Looking Forward

This book will, I hope, deepen your understanding of yourself and others. In ceasing to look only for simple 'types' you will learn how to use birth order as an invaluable starting point to help you unravel the complexity of human character: why people hold the attitudes and beliefs that they do and how these came to be. In turn, you should achieve a greater awareness of your own strengths and shortcomings, and be equipped to make wiser decisions in future because you know yourself better. Most importantly, I hope that you'll find it easier to feel proud of and capitalise on your unique qualities and, ultimately, become more self-confident.

# PART ONE

# The Four Main Birth-order Positions

# First Borns

We begin not only with the first child in the family, but also with the most common birth-order position. The modern trend is to have smaller families, so of course that's not surprising. It's estimated that in 2010 nearly 40 per cent of individuals in the UK were first borns, and that this figure will rise to 50 per cent before long. Perhaps, then, it's understandable that more articles and book chapters have been dedicated to first borns than those in any other birth-order position.

However, the problem is that as first borns your 'special' characteristics seem to be so numerous, and cover so many areas of functioning, that you might wonder what it is that sets you apart from anyone else! Therefore, in order to identify those characteristics that distinguish first borns, I'll start by taking a look at what is likely to have been happening when you were growing up – in particular, what was distinctive about your upbringing and what differentiates you from your brothers and sisters.

## Your Family Environment

The birth of a first child is an overwhelming experience for parents. Of course, the birth of each child is unique and precious, but parental feelings are particularly powerful when the entire process is new as well. Just take a look, for example, at the number of photographs and mementoes your parents have for their first born compared to the other children in the family. It's fairly safe to conclude that most first borns start life in the care of parents who considered their existence to be a joyful miracle. However, the uniqueness of that situation will have had negative as well as positive consequences.

On the positive side, the extra time and attention your parents bestowed upon you meant that you were held, attended to and talked to a great deal, almost certainly more than any of your younger siblings. You will have had more chances to hear language and to observe adult – that is, more mature – social interactions. These opportunities to hear your native language and to practise responding to it when you were young, are likely to have made it easier for you now to communicate well and to relate skilfully to other people, helping you in a number of ways. In particular, the ability to express yourself clearly means that you probably did well in school and were better placed to reach your potential academically.

On the negative side, however, it must be remembered that your parents were novices. They'd never been parents before, and even if they'd looked after children in some other capacity, you were their first 'full-time' childcare job, as well as the first child they'd looked after who was truly their own. This almost inevitably means that they were more nervous when they cared for you, and because babies and children are acutely sensitive to their carers' mood state, there's a good chance that at some level, you were aware of this anxiety. This is likely to have made you more anxious than you might have been with more experienced parents.

Remember, too, that you started life almost exclusively in the company of adults. Because we tend to measure ourselves in terms of those people we're around most often, early on you may have established the habit of comparing yourself to individuals who were already far more capable than you were. The consequence is that you probably set high expectations for yourself – often unrealistically high – and that as a result you frequently feel disappointed in your achievements, even when to many onlookers you're doing extremely well.

Thus, the environment you were born into offered you many advantages in the form of lots of attention, rich exposure to language and opportunities to observe good social skills in action, but also some disadvantages, such as relatively little scope to feel more capable than others and a rather anxious atmosphere when you were growing up.

## Typical Characteristics of a First Born

These are the characteristics that most often distinguish a first born:

### First borns have a strong desire to gain the approval of others, particularly those in positions of authority

Like singles, as well as last borns who come along much later than the sibling who preceded them, you first borns have a period of time when you enjoy the exclusive attention of your parents. However, unlike singles and those 'late' last borns, sooner or later you lose that exclusivity. That is, at some point, you have to start sharing what you'd previously considered to be your own. Because this important loss is usually experienced early on – within the first four years of your life and, therefore, before your own sense of place in the family and of security was firmly established – your thirst for approval will probably always feel unquenchable. In other words, sadly, no matter how much praise or adoration you receive, you're likely still to find yourself wanting more.

However, for any number of reasons – perhaps because you were anxious not to annoy your parents by letting them know how needy you were feeling, or perhaps because you simply couldn't figure out how to wrest their attention away from your new brother or sister – you may have begun to widen your search for adult praise and approval. Soon, anyone who occupied a position of power would become someone you wanted to please – because, of course, anyone in power is, in effect, a parental figure.

On a similar note, you're also liable to feel easily hurt by any criticism that's levelled at you by an authority figure. This is again linked to your loss of exclusive parental attention. A criticism can feel very much like a rejection, and it's therefore likely to trigger your underlying anxiety about being supplanted by someone else in the eyes of those who are in charge of your wellbeing. These feelings are particularly distressing for many first borns because they are unaware of why they're feeling so upset.

## First borns are law-abiding and conservative, and accepting and respectful of existing rules and regulations

If you're keen to please those in authority, it follows that you'll accept the rules they've set and identify with their values. It follows, too, that it's less likely that you will break the law and more so that you'll be aware of and respect social mores and community regulations.

You first borns also tend to be more conservative in your outlook. You value traditions and are apt to look up to the older established and well-known members of society. New ideas and innovations may feel more threatening to you than they do to individuals in other birth-order positions. As a result, you're more likely to stick with what you know rather than take your chances with new and unproven schemes and ideas.

## First borns want to be in charge and 'in control' and to take up positions of leadership

Not only do you admire those in power, many of you also want to be just like them – in other words, to assume power yourself. This may not, unfortunately, be for the best of motives! When any of us loses something that's really important to us – in your case, the full attention of your parent(s) – a common way of dealing with this is to become the giver ourselves of what we feel we've lost. That's why some first borns endlessly seek positions that carry greater and greater power. However, because the need you're trying to address is rooted in the past, you never feel satisfied. Instead, you'll go on trying to find yet more ways to exert authority – and that hungry searching will, in turn, bring with it new difficulties. That's because once you've gained the position you were so certain you wanted, you're then, of course, highly vulnerable to criticism. A vicious and exhausting circle can easily become established because most of the time people in power will conclude that the only way to curtail such criticism is to assume even more power!

It takes great insight to be able to step back from this anxious search for reassurance and outside affirmation and to look within yourself for the praise and reassurance you're seeking. Sadly, few people ever acquire this degree of wisdom and self-assurance.

The fact is that a disproportionate number of first borns are in leadership positions. For example, more US presidents and British prime ministers have been first borns than would be expected statistically, and the same is true of the CEOs of most companies and organisations.

## First borns tend to be academically successful

You're good students in the traditional sense. You do your homework and generally accept what your teachers – who are authority figures, after all – tell you without question. Individuals in other birth-order positions often obtain high marks in school too, of course. But the difference lies in the reason.

You first borns are driven primarily to please your parents and teachers (although as you become engrossed in the material you may well become fascinated by the subject in its own right). Later borns, on the other hand, most often choose to study something largely because it interests them, and it is this interest that encourages them at least as much as any desire to please their teachers and parents.

Another reason why first borns do well in school is that they tend to have superior language skills. As we've seen, because you were the only child when you were learning to talk, your parents would have had more time to speak to you. You'll therefore have had numerous opportunities to hear your native language spoken clearly and well. You would also have been listened to more than your younger brothers and sisters. Given that academic success depends so much on the ability to comprehend language and to communicate clearly, such well-developed linguistic skills provide a tremendous advantage at school.

## First borns are usually organised and responsible

As you'd imagine, by the time you've grown up you'll have had a great deal of practice taking on positions of responsibility for others. You watched your parents and other carers when they looked after your younger siblings, so you observed repeatedly how to look after others as well as how to organise and run a household. No doubt you were also given a number of opportunities to practise being efficient and responsible yourself, because your parents probably needed your help!

All this practice and observation served you well when you were growing up. Your organisational skills and your obvious competence when it comes to taking charge are likely to make others want to put you in control. Furthermore, because you're quite used to expecting that others will need your help, you're usually the first person to step up and volunteer to give that help when there's work to be done. You also tend to be the one who organises others and goads them into action when a group effort is required.

If you couple this sort of behaviour with a good command of language, you can begin to understand why first borns have little difficulty convincing others to put them in positions of leadership – and that, of course, suits you well, because it's generally where you want to be.

## First borns are nurturing and caring

You're the ones who are most likely to take on caring roles in adulthood – you'll often choose careers that involve looking after and/or educating others. This is, of course, in part because you're so familiar with and experienced in carrying out these roles. However, it's also true that you seek out such positions because they're associated in your mind with receiving praise and attention from authority figures.

Most of you are, however, rather selective about the *type* of caring role you'll take on. You're more inclined to nurture and to teach in well-established, mainstream ways rather than to choose less conventional means to help others. So for example, you might become teachers, nurses and doctors, rather than train as herbalists or reflexologists.

\*   \*   \*

Thus far, the picture of first-born characteristics is reasonably encouraging, or at least not disagreeable. Although the birth of a first born is generally considered little short of a miracle and you probably received lots of loving care and attention, the consequences for your character development are not, as I said earlier, all good. Here are two less positive traits that the first child in the family must contend with:

## First borns tend to be highly self-critical and less likely to forgive themselves when they make mistakes

You dread failure, and you never wish to be thought of as lacking in good qualities. As you've probably already guessed, this characteristic is driven by your fear of rejection. Because you ask so much of yourself and because you take so much personal responsibility for the way others see you, it also means you're not likely to forgive yourself easily when you don't manage to do what was asked of you – or even more so, when you fail to meet your own lofty expectations.

I suspect that such harsh self-criticism is particularly true if the brother or sister who comes next is born quite soon after you were – that is, before you lost the belief that you're responsible for everything that happens. All children think this way when they're very young, and until they're about four or five, their first reaction when things go wrong is to assume responsibility. As they mature, however, children gradually learn to look for reasons outside themselves when things go wrong or change. What this means is that, although you won't remember it very well, you were devastated when that new baby arrived and you no longer had your parents to yourself. If you were still very young, you'd have been unable to understand what was happening. Unless your parents reassured you repeatedly that you were a 'good' girl or boy and that they still loved you, too, you'd have concluded that they now preferred the new baby because you were now less likeable in some way. Many first borns never lose this tendency to feel guilty and/or overly responsible when things go wrong.

You wouldn't have reacted quite so strongly to the arrival of a new sibling if you'd been a bit older when the baby first arrived – if you were, say, at least five. By then, you'd have developed cognitively to the point that you were capable of realising that the arrival of the new baby wasn't because you were suddenly inadequate or that you'd done anything wrong. None the less, you would still probably have felt jealous and left out – unless, that is, your parents were incredibly sensitive and managed to find ways that allowed you to feel helpful and still just as important.

Another aspect of the first born's tendency to anxiety and over-responsibility is that you find it hard to delegate responsibility, even when what you've been asked to do means you become overloaded, stressed and fatigued. You prefer to stay in control even when it wears you out, because you're so afraid that if you lose that control, things might go wrong – and that if they do, you'll have only yourself to blame.

It is possible to change this exhausting attitude towards life and to learn to delegate work and to trust others to do a good job, too. However, because the habit of over-responsibility is usually so well established, you may decide that some counselling or therapy would help you to learn how to let go and start to believe that things won't fall apart just because you're not totally in charge.

## First borns are more likely than others to feel stressed and to seek psychological help

You're more prone than other people to suffer from anxiety and, in particular, feelings of insecurity and jealousy. I think that by now you've already understood how this comes about – as a result of the loss of that exclusive parental attention in your early years.

Feelings of displacement and jealousy make a deep impression, particularly if they first arise when you're still quite young, if the new sibling is difficult to settle and soothe or if either or both parents are already stressed or exhausted for other reasons and therefore appear distant or less caring for a time.

That doesn't, of course, mean that all first borns are bound to be anxious, insecure and jealous! It simply means that you're relatively more likely to be so than your siblings because of the circumstances in which you grew up. How strong and how lasting this tendency is depends on individual temperament and how your parents handled the arrival of your new sibling. I'll be examining these factors in greater detail in Part Two, in particular when considering the effect your parents had on you (see pages 101–17).

One other reason why there's more chance that you will seek psychological help is that first borns generally hold authority figures in unquestionable high regard. Therefore, when you're in distress – as most of us will be from time to time, regardless of birth-order position – you're more likely than others to assume that some authority figure (in this case, a GP, a psychiatrist, a counsellor or a psychologist) will know how to help.

## The First Born's Guide to Choosing a Partner

Birth order is, of course, only one of a number of factors to consider when thinking about what makes a good partnership. Overall, if two people love and respect one another and are absolutely determined to make their relationship work, it will, regardless of either one's birth-order profile. None the less, knowing each other's birth order helps when predicting how difficult or easy it will be to get along.

The maxim that 'opposites attract' makes a good starting point when we consider the best birth-order partnerships. For example, a first born and a last born very often make a good match: the organised and caring first born wants someone to keep in order and to nurture, and the fun-loving but rather less organised and more dependent last born is likely to respond well to someone who offers these qualities.

Middle borns also make good partners for first borns because those in the middle are used to allowing someone else to take charge. However, if a first born is particularly powerful, their middle-born partner may feel rather over-dominated and unable to express themselves (although because of their own particular birth-order characteristics – see pages 32–52 – they may not voice their dissatisfaction). If you feel that you have a tendency to dominate and direct others and your partner's a middle born, try to step back at times and ask your partner for their opinion or encourage them to express their concerns.

Among the most difficult partnerships tend to be those of two first borns or of a first born and a single. When both of you want to be in charge, particularly if you're both highly competitive, conflict is extremely likely. These matches *can* work well – but only if each partner genuinely respects the qualities of the other, and at least one of them expresses their desire to lead and dominate somewhere *outside* the relationship. If this applies to you, try to cultivate some independent interests where you can put your leadership qualities to good use and, at the same time, take some pressure off your relationship.

# The First Born's Guide to Choosing a Career

It must be obvious by now that the best choice of work for you is the sort that allows you to take as much responsibility as you can comfortably handle. Having said that, and although you may not think so, you'll also do best and feel happiest in a career where there's someone who keeps a check on your tendency to take on too much, to do everything *too* perfectly and to push yourself relentlessly. Otherwise, you're prone to burnout. Furthermore, the sense of failure that accompanies that burnout will hit you first borns particularly hard.

Your work will feel most satisfying if it provides you with some opportunities to teach or in some way to care for others. In addition, well-established, conventional, tried-and-true methods will probably appeal to you – mainstream jobs in health care and education are good examples.

There is a disproportionate number of first borns in leadership roles in politics and business. If you have made this choice and it had more to do with the desire for power than because the actual work itself appealed to you, you're less likely to feel fulfilled or satisfied at work. It's important, therefore, to evaluate carefully the content of the work you'll be doing, rather than choosing a job based on the amount of power you'll command.

---

### *Famous first borns*

- Richard Branson
- J. K. Rowling
- Benito Mussolini
- Oprah Winfrey

## CASE STUDY: **Simon**

Simon was thirty-seven when he referred himself to me for what he described as 'serial burnout'. Since his first job at the age of twenty-one he'd never been unemployed, but neither had he stayed in a job for more than three years. 'Either the job disappoints me, or else I know I'm letting people down at work,' he told me.

He'd been married twice and divorced once, and was now living on his own. He described his two former partners as 'rather similar – perhaps too much so. Perhaps I didn't learn my lesson the first time.' Both were highly intelligent and ambitious. His first wife Jane was a solicitor. His second wife Amanda ran an HR department. Amanda had left him recently after six years because, she said, she wanted children and he didn't. 'Actually,' Simon told me, 'I do want to have kids, but it never seems to be the right time.' Both women had complained that Simon was too controlling – Jane had even accused him of 'wrapping her in cotton wool'. When I asked Simon whether he thought this might have been true, he admitted that he did, perhaps, come on too strong. 'But I thought women want to be taken care of,' he added defensively.

Simon was the eldest of three boys. He described his mother as 'timid and shy. I never knew how she was really feeling – but I think now she must have been rather depressed.' She'd trained as a primary school teacher, but hadn't taught since Simon was born. He described his father as 'a tyrant, really. Whenever he said anything, we all jumped, especially mum.' He owned his own company, and had become extremely wealthy. All three boys had attended public school, and all had gone to university.

I asked Simon to tell me more about his brothers. 'Well,

there's my younger brother Will,' he said. 'I'd describe him as happy-go-lucky. Nothing ever bothers him and everything always seems to go his way. I'd be jealous of him if I didn't like him so much.' Will had married Jen and they'd moved to Melbourne, so Simon didn't see him often. When I asked about his other brother, Simon's face darkened. 'I really can't stand Tom. He's so . . . well, so *perfect.*'

Tom was only fifteen months younger than Simon. 'Tom is dad's favourite – he always has been. And dad made it so obvious.' Tom had read economics at university, but then returned – on his father's invitation – to their home town to take over the business. He was married with two children, and was apparently very happy.

Simon had done well at school, and at university he achieved a First. He'd been active in sports and in a number of societies, and he was described by teachers and friends alike as a 'natural leader'.

When I asked him about his career path, he laughed. 'I was so idealistic, but also, not very focused. I wanted to change things – that's what I felt – but I hadn't thought about how I'd do that. At the same time, I felt I wanted to make a lot of money.' He'd applied for a number of jobs and had been offered all of them. 'I just chose the one that paid the highest salary – not a very admirable person, was I?' he said ruefully. He'd met Jane at university, they married on graduating and moved to London to start work.

After only six months, Simon felt restless and disappointed in his job as a stock jobber: 'How can you enjoy spending all that money if you're totally drained every day by your work?' On an impulse, he contacted one of the other companies that had offered him a job at university. Fortunately for him, the offer was reinstated, and, with high hopes, he began work in a firm of building contractors.

His remit was to work with overseas charities to build schools in impoverished areas.

Simon described this as the best job he'd had during the last sixteen years. However, he left after two and a half years because, he said, 'I didn't know what I was doing, really. They deserved better.' This was in spite of the fact that he'd been offered a substantial pay rise to stay on. He told me that he wished now he had stayed on. At the time, he wondered if he might have been depressed – he'd just learned that his wife was having an affair and he was drinking heavily.

There then followed a series of short-term contracts, none of which satisfied him. Six years ago he'd taken a job with another building firm and he'd met Amanda. They married after eighteen months, although by that time he was bored at work and was looking for other employment. Six months ago and three jobs later, he and Amanda separated.

After hearing this history, I asked Simon to close his eyes and imagine that he was giving a speech at a reception that marked his retirement. I urged him not to think carefully, but simply to react to whatever came to mind. To his surprise, he said he'd seen himself in a school. 'I'm a teacher. Just a teacher, not a headmaster – not even head of department. Just a teacher.' He seemed confused and embarrassed by this. 'What's there to be proud of about that? I'd probably be making almost nothing, and anyway I shouldn't be wasting my time in a female-dominated field.'

I asked Simon who'd told him that teaching was a waste of time. 'Any job where women dominate shouldn't be considered a proper profession,' he asserted. I pointed out his use of 'should', and explained that when someone says he 'should' do or believe something, it's usually because he feels obligated to do so to please someone else, rather than because he really believes it. This seemed to strike home, because at that point Simon interrupted me. 'No wonder mum was depressed! Dad was always putting down her qualifications!' So was Simon's avoidance of teaching an attempt to please his father and avoid his criticism? Was teaching in truth something he might enjoy? Was his love of education perhaps part of the reason he'd so enjoyed the job involving building schools?

This was the breakthrough Simon needed. During the next few sessions, he realised that the value system he'd constructed to measure a job's worth – that is, how much money he could make – was an attempt to please his father. In truth, Simon wanted to make learning come alive for others because he'd loved learning and studying hard himself at school and at university. However, he knew his father would scoff at his choice of a 'woman's job'.

It took Simon three months more to pluck up the courage to apply for a teaching course at a nearby university. He was accepted immediately for the course that would begin in ten months' time – adequate time, he reckoned, to put enough money aside so he could afford the time out to retrain.

He'd also begun talking to Amanda again, and they were considering cautiously the possibility of getting back together. Simon said she'd brought up the issue of starting a family, and that in many ways he felt that now was still a bad time. 'On the other hand,' he said, 'I'm beginning to see that if you wait for the perfect time to do something, you wait for ever.'

By this time, Simon was feeling, by his own account, 'happier than I've ever been'. His father had, just as he'd predicted, dismissed his new plans as 'a sign of depression'. His mother, however, was so delighted that she'd praised Simon directly in the face of her husband's disapproval. Both Will, and surprisingly, Tom, were very supportive of his decision too. In fact, Tom told Simon that he'd always wondered why he hadn't chosen teaching in the first place because he was such a natural.

## What Simon's experience tells us

Simon's struggle illustrates well the problems that can beset a first born. As a child, he'd no doubt helped his mother, who was herself struggling because of her depression, to look after his younger brothers. He'd gained great satisfaction in this role and probably revelled in his mother's approval. However, he also wanted very much to please his father – a man who openly dismissed careers in education or other sorts of 'caring' as fit only for women. Therefore, in a confused attempt to please, Simon had adopted his father's value system and had used his academic success to win him jobs that earned him a great deal of money. Then, because these jobs didn't satisfy him, he began a restless search for one that would – still, unfortunately, measuring each one's worth only by the salary it offered.

Meanwhile, Simon had transferred his (unsatisfied) desire to care for and nurture others to his personal life, making the two women he married feel overprotected and over-controlled. Finally, by setting impossibly high standards for the 'right' time to have children, he'd also made Amanda feel – probably quite rightly – that, for him, there would never be a 'right' time to start a family.

In therapy, Simon realised that if he simply tried to please his father, he would never feel fulfilled; also that he couldn't please both his parents simultaneously, anyway. He also began to understand that there's no point in looking for a 'perfect' time to start a family – or, for that matter, to embark on any other major life change. This helped him to understand his wife's point of view and to resume contact with her in an attempt to work through their differences.

## CASE STUDY: Laura

It took Laura three weeks to decide to make an appointment to see me after her GP suggested that she would benefit from some short-term therapy. She was sixty-seven and had been retired for just over a year. She'd worked for a small but thriving local firm as the company secretary for over forty-two years when she stepped down.

Laura had been reluctant to leave, but she wasn't interested in adapting to the new technologies that the company had embraced, and she also suffered from chronic pain that had begun to make it difficult to sit for any length of time. Immediately after retirement she'd had surgery on her hips and, as a result, was virtually free from pain. To her surprise, however, her depression – this was what her GP had diagnosed – had only deepened. She'd tried antidepressant medication but suffered badly from side effects and had given it up. Finally, she decided to try a course of therapy.

Laura was the elder of two girls. Her younger sister Janet had married directly after leaving school and raised four boys. Janet had never sought paid work, and Laura told me she'd always been fairly carefree and easy-going. They were friendly and kept in touch, but because Janet had moved to Scotland when she married they only met up on holidays.

Laura, on the other hand, had been a studious and serious child. She'd worked hard in school, and then went to London to secretarial college. Although she'd done very well in her course and had been offered several jobs in London, she chose to return to work in her home town – she said city life hadn't suited her.

Laura had had a number of boyfriends before she met Tom at work. They'd become engaged after two years and had set a wedding date when he was killed in a car crash. After that loss, she never married. She told me that Tom was 'the one', and she knew no one could replace him. None the less, she was very sociable. She went out often with friends, sang in a local choir, was an active member of her church and gave time to various charities.

As Laura's parents became increasingly frail she had looked after them. Her father had died six years before she first saw me and her mother two years later. In her last year, her mother had moved in with Laura because she needed constant care. Laura told me that she believed she'd grieved both of these losses completely with the strong support of her vicar. She did admit, however, that she felt there had been a 'hole' in her life since her mother's death that she didn't know how to fill.

Laura began her first session with a torrent of apologies: she didn't want to put anyone out; she was sorry to be such a nuisance. I asked her how she saw herself – did she often feel that she was a nuisance to others? She told me that until she'd retired, she'd felt fulfilled and happy. She knew she was good at her job and that she was valued at work, and she knew how much she'd helped her parents. But now that all the work and the caring was over, she said she just felt useless.

Over the next few sessions, Laura began to talk about how she'd always compared herself to Janet: how she'd wanted to be easy-going like her, and not to feel the need to gain approval from others, particularly her colleagues. When it fell upon her to look after her parents because she was the nearer of the two sisters, she explained that she'd actually felt good about the responsibility. She'd always felt her parents found Janet the easier child, and she was glad to be able to do something they truly appreciated.

It took some time, but gradually Laura began to

entertain the idea that it might be acceptable for her to direct some of her energies and sense of responsibility towards herself, rather than others. She also realised that she wasn't necessarily 'useless' when she wasn't caring for someone or doing work she'd been assigned. In addition, Laura learned to praise herself, instead of feeling that the only praise worth having came from others. Gradually, the sense of 'uselessness' that had defined her depression was replaced by self-acceptance.

## What Laura's experience tells us

When Laura first came to see me, she showed all the classic characteristics of a first born: she'd been responsible and acted conventionally all her life; she'd excelled in education; she was dutiful and looked after others. However, she'd neglected to take enough care of herself. She had not considered whether she was happy and fulfilled in what she was doing – instead, she'd relied for too long on gaining praise and approval from others. As she learned to give herself the same care and attention she'd always extended to other people, Laura began to feel happier and more at ease with herself.

## First Borns in a Nutshell

To sum up, here are the characteristics most often associated with first borns:

- Keen to please others, particularly those in positions of authority

- Likely to stick to the rules and to accept received wisdom, rather than follow up radical ideas and theories

- More likely than others to take on positions of responsibility and leadership

- Apt to do relatively well at school

- Almost certainly dutiful, organised and responsible

- Nurturing and caring, and likely to offer to look after others

- Apt to set high standards and expectations, and to be highly self-critical

- Prone to worry and in particular to feel jealous and guilty, and to seek professional help for their problems

Now let's take a look at the younger siblings in the family.

# Chapter Two

# Middle Borns

More myths seem to surround middle borns than those in any other birth-order position. The middle born is usually portrayed as 'a difficult person', 'the black sheep of the family' or someone who's unhappy, rebellious and withdrawn – the odd one out. Yet when you examine the statistics and when you talk to middle borns, the picture is actually quite different. Although some of these stereotypical descriptions may occasionally apply, for the most part middle borns have been misrepresented.

To create a more accurate picture and draw up a list of the characteristics associated with you middle borns, we need to start by examining the circumstances in which you grew up.

## Your Family Environment

Before we examine your family environment in detail, it's worth noting a potential complication when trying to create a picture of the typical middle born. Those middle children who are the second in a family of three are not only and always a middle child, of course. They're also in the 'last born' position until the third child comes along. If a third child is born relatively soon after the second – say, within three years – then they'll have little, if any, opportunity to function as a last born. However, if there's a large age gap between the second and third child, it's likely that the second child will have some qualities that are typical of both a middle and a last born. Therefore, if you are a middle born, but your next sibling is more than three years younger than you, you're advised to read both this chapter and the one on last borns (see pages 53–74). That said, let's turn now to the typical family environment in which the middle child grows up.

Those of you in the middle of the family have a great advantage over first borns because you were raised by more experienced parents. The birth of the first child always receives more attention than later births, so your arrival will have received less than that of your elder sibling, it's true. At the same time, however, your parents were more relaxed and confident about what they were doing – much more so than they were with their first child, so you were doubtless treated in a calmer and more matter-of-fact manner. This means you're likely to be less of a worrier than your older sister or brother.

You're probably more socially skilled than your older sibling as well. That's because you had to work harder than he or she did to be noticed by your parents – and for human infants, parental attention is vital because it's the only way their basic needs are met. From the moment you were born, you had to share your parents with an older sibling, and before too long with a new baby as well. You lacked the advantage of maturity so that meant your older sibling could do most things better than you could, and after a time you were no longer the needy and adorable baby. That meant that when you were growing up you probably had to be quite innovative to find ways that would attract and hold your parents' attention.

The situation would have been particularly difficult for you if you and your siblings are all the same gender, because you couldn't even make use of that difference to distinguish yourself! You would also have had to look for ways to gain adult attention that didn't incur the jealous retaliation of your older sibling. Therefore, more than any other child in the family, you grew up socially smart – that is, knowing how to draw enough attention to yourself to get what you need, but without annoying others by stealing the spotlight from them.

With that feature as our anchor point, let's look more closely at the qualities that most often describe a middle born.

## Typical Characteristics of a Middle Born

These are the characteristics that most often distinguish a middle child:

### Middle borns are able to get along with most people and to restore social harmony when conflict arises

Middle borns are the co-operators. You're the diplomats who come up with compromises and figure out how to smooth the waters when everyone's at war. You manage to get on well with most people and to fit into any group, classroom or office in which you find yourself. You are, more than anything else, peer-centred – that is, you're very aware of and sensitive to the needs and feelings of the people you're with.

When people get locked into arguments and everyone stubbornly stands their own ground, you're likely to be the one who tries to think of a way to sort things out. After all, more often than not that was your role when you were growing up. Sandwiched between two siblings who both wanted things done very much their own way and for their own reasons, you would probably be the one who proposed a reasonable compromise. Quite often, however, that compromise would be at your own expense, because if someone had to give that little bit more, you were the one who usually did so.

Don't, however, confuse your willingness to compromise with the 'Let's sort you all out' behaviour of first borns. Both first and middle borns tend to be the ones who sort out group differences. First borns, however, do so by taking charge, by leading and by offering solutions, whereas middle borns are more likely to suggest compromises and then give the most ground so that an agreement can be reached.

## Middle borns are easily persuaded by others, and most likely to give in to peer pressure

Another distinction – this one less subtle – between first borns and those of you who are in the middle is the group you identify yourself with. Middle borns are most attuned to their peers. Having grown up surrounded by other children, your primary focus has always been those who are roughly your age.

This particular characteristic has both an up-side and a down-side for you. On the one hand you're able to find ways to get along socially in most situations and with most people. However, you're also more likely to find yourself in trouble if the people you're with are looking to challenge authority or to make mischief. This will be particularly true if you're impulsive because it means you'll be inclined simply to follow the crowd rather than first stopping and thinking about whether it's wise to do so.

## Middle borns are more likely to have an accurate view of what they can achieve, and to be able to set realistic expectations for themselves

Because you grew up always with other children around you, some a bit older and more capable than you and others younger and less mature, your model of comparison is based as much on peers as it is on adults. That means that the expectations you'll have for yourself are likely to have been more or less appropriate for your chronological age and developmental level. Because your standards are peer-based, they're therefore more likely to be realistic.

Your basis of comparison when you consider your strengths and weaknesses stands in strong contrast to that of first borns, who compare themselves to and base their standards primarily on adult (parental) behaviour and expectations. It is also different from the way last borns see themselves. Last borns compare themselves almost entirely to individuals who are already more competent than they are because, of course, everyone else they see around them in their family is older and more capable.

## Middle borns are likely to excel in slightly more creative ways – sport, art or music, for example

You middle borns will almost certainly focus your energies in areas where your older sibling hasn't been particularly successful – and if you think about the family in the way that Charles Darwin did, it's easy to see why. Darwin came up with an explanation for the differences between siblings that's known as the Principle of Divergence. We'll be using this principle repeatedly throughout the book, with regard in particular to you and to last borns.

Darwin was fascinated by the characteristics that allowed some creatures to flourish, as compared to others who languished or died out. He reasoned that in any given environment the resources will be limited, and that everyone in that environment knows this at some level and will, therefore, try to get hold of as big a share as they possibly can. In the environment that is the family, the most valuable resource – that is, the one that allows a child to grow up safe and strong – is parental care and attention.

Because young children (and most young mammals, for that matter) are fairly helpless when they're born, they need their carers to gather food for them and to provide them with shelter and protection for some time at least, until they're strong enough and experienced enough to do these things for themselves. Humans require this help for a relatively longer period of time than any other creature. Human babies need, therefore, to find ways to endear themselves to their carers – that is, to make themselves noticeable and very, very lovable. They're programmed to encourage their carers to pay attention to them, make sacrifices for them and to look after them especially well.

Of course, parents are genetically predisposed to care for their offspring in turn, because it allows them (through the genetic material they've passed on to their children) to 'survive' beyond their own life span. However, although parents will make every effort to care for and protect all of their children, they can only do so much. Each child will, therefore, try their utmost to seem as important and special to their parents as possible, to ensure that they are the first person their parents think of if they have to make choices about whom to help most.

If you, as a middle child, had tried to gain your parents' attention in the same way that your older sibling did – say, by doing well in school or perhaps by being particularly clever with words – then you'd most likely have remained unnoticed. That's because your elder sibling would already have been more mature and capable than you were and could take the spotlight off you.

In addition, that older brother or sister would also have had a head start figuring out how best to please your parents. That meant the most likely – and that's usually the most conventional – way to please them was no longer an option for you. In our society, the most conventional way to please parents is to do well in school. Your older sibling had probably cornered that method, so you would have had to think of a new and different way to gain that much-needed parental attention and approval. The most common second choices that please parents are sport or the arts.

This is why, by the way, in larger families – where there are four or more children – you notice such big differences between the children. In fact, many psychologists argue that you'll find bigger differences between children in the same family than you'll find if you compare children from different families with one another! That may sound surprising, but when you stop to think about it, it makes sense. After all, each child in any given family is trying their utmost to distinguish themselves from their brothers and sisters, something they don't need to do so much with their peers.

## Middle borns are often the first child in the family to leave home, or at least the one who leaves home at the youngest age

It's not clear why this is so often true of the middle born. Perhaps it's because you grew tired of always compromising and standing aside for the sake of others. Perhaps it's because you imagined that your opportunities would be better in the wider social world than in the family home. It might even be that, because you were confident that you could get on almost anywhere, you yielded to the spirit of adventure that's natural in the young. Whatever the reason, middle borns tend to leave home relatively earlier than do their siblings.

## Middle borns are more likely than others to take up 'causes' and to support 'crusades' for the downtrodden

Middle borns put a great deal of effort into keeping the social wheels greased, as we've already learned. This is great – *for everyone else.* However, for you there's a cost. Your efforts on behalf of the family or group you're with leave you less time to ensure that your own needs are met. Also, because there were fewer opportunities for you to have special time and attention with your parents alone, as there was almost always someone else around, after a time, you may even have become less aware of what your own needs and wishes were. After all, you probably thought, why think about what I'd really like if the odds of realising my dreams are so small?

However, even though you didn't think about your own aspirations consciously, it didn't mean that your frustration about not realising your dreams went away. Instead, your sense of injustice was probably repressed and made inaccessible to your conscious mind, and later 'projected' – that is, ascribed to other people – elsewhere. In other words, when you use projection, you single out a person or group of people and assume that they're troubled by the same worries or problems as you. That's why, I suspect, you see so many middle borns taking up the cause of the underdog and helping those in need. Whether you're conscious of it or not, what you're saying is, in effect: 'We all deserve equal treatment. I'm not going to overlook someone just because they're not crying out for their needs to be met! I'm going to help them – just as I would like to have been noticed and helped, too.'

## Middle borns often express their individuality in unusual ways, particularly during adolescence

Another consequence of compromising your own needs in the interests of social harmony is that after a time, you're likely to start feeling resentful. However, instead of asserting yourself and trying to make changes as would a first born, or using charm or cunning to get others to give you what you want as would a last born, your pent-up resentment is more likely to show itself in the way you present yourself. The middle born is the one in the family who's most likely to dress bizarrely, to sport extreme hairstyles or wear unusual makeup, particularly during the teenage years when all children are trying to carve out their individual identity. This is the middle born's way of saying, 'Hey, look at me! Come on, *notice me!*'

Thus far, the description of middle borns has been fairly positive, or at worst neutral. We have a picture of someone who's generally good at fitting in and getting along with others, someone who's able to be independent at a fairly young age, a person who's realistic when assessing their own talents and abilities and able by themselves to carve out their own niche and express their individuality.

Is there, however, any negative aspect to this birth-order position? Judging from my clinical experience, I'd say that there definitely is:

## Middle borns are frequently plagued by a lack of direction, in part because they have trouble recognising what they really want

Although statistically middle borns are least likely to seek psychological help, I've found that when they do, their complaints are often initially rather vague. They're most often referred with symptoms of depression or anxiety – tiredness, a lack of direction, panicky feelings and a sense of gloom and doom about the future. At the same time, however, they're often unclear about how or why their distress has come about. Moreover – and this really does single out middle borns – they find it hard to imagine what life will be like when they're free of symptoms.

Perhaps this is because you middle borns have become so accustomed to downplaying your own dreams and desires that after a time, you've lost awareness of them. In addition, when you were young you may have deliberately hidden your most heartfelt dreams and desires from your older sibling in particular, because you were afraid that he or she might laugh at you or take advantage of knowing what you most wanted. After a time of repressing your wishes repeatedly, they were pushed out of your conscious mind and you were no longer aware of them.

Whatever the explanation, if patients tell me they're feeling low and directionless, but that simultaneously they have little or no conscious idea of what they'd do if they were free of this distress, then it's quite likely they're middle borns. Our work together most often centres on helping them to discover their own true passions and talents and encouraging them to accept that they have the same right as anyone else to develop and express their dreams and desires.

## The Middle Born's Guide to Choosing a Partner

Your partners are lucky. Because of your long history of negotiating (sibling) conflict and making compromises for the sake of others, most people find you easy to get along with. That means you'll be able to have a successful relationship with someone in any other birth-order position.

You middle borns make excellent partners for first borns and singles because you're happy to allow them to take charge and make decisions. You're good with last borns as well, because you'll tolerate their need to be the centre of attention and because you're likely to agree to any of their adventures or to any unconventional ways of living that they might propose. You can have a successful relationship with another middle born as well, although the two of you may be so deferential that you'll have difficulty making up your minds!

However, your malleability could bring with it some problems. If you *never* stand up for yourself, *never* hold your position firmly, it's possible that your partner will lose some respect for you. He or she might also start taking advantage of your deference, and after a time you might feel (quite rightly) that your needs are being totally ignored. It's important, therefore, that you take time, periodically, to think about what's most important to you and – at least with regard to those issues – that you stand firm about what you want for yourself. Try to notice when something intrigues you or excites your interest, and make sure you tell your partner. Be direct and clear.

## The Middle Born's Guide to Choosing a Career

Middle borns are generally more comfortable working as part of a team than they are working alone. You're used to being in groups – in your family, it's all you knew, really – and you can be relied on to keep things running smoothly. That means, of course, that you're a welcome member of almost any team. You work well alongside most other people, and you're also willing to take on work that others expect from you with little questioning or complaint.

However, therein lies the potential for your own dissatisfaction in the workplace. Because you're so accepting and so accommodating, others may take advantage of you. You're liable, therefore, to find yourself working harder and longer than you should.

If you feel you're particularly vulnerable to this tendency, be sure to choose who you work for carefully. Look for a company that checks up regularly on the satisfaction of its employees, and try to find one that has a good HR (human resources) team, so you have people to talk to if you feel you're being overlooked or overworked.

On the other hand, you could of course work alone – either for yourself or in a job where you're the only one in a particular position. However, this may not come as easily to you as it would, say, to a single. You may find it more difficult to motivate yourself when there's no one else around to make suggestions about setting goals or maintaining the drive necessary to achieve them.

Finally, although it's true that you can fit in almost anywhere, you're likely to feel most fulfilled if at least some of your work aims to promote the causes or address the needs of those who are less privileged and advantaged.

## Famous middle borns

- Tony Blair
- Bill Gates
- Stella McCartney
- Princess Diana

## CASE STUDY: Diane

Diane was referred to me because she was experiencing panic attacks at work. She'd felt rather panicky at times for many years, but during the last three months she'd begun to have full-blown attacks, and these had become so frequent that she was beginning to wonder whether she'd have to give up work.

She'd been working as a company secretary for the same firm for ten years. The idea of giving up work was particularly worrying to her because the money she earned was the only steady income in the family. Her husband, Robert, was self-employed and his earnings were extremely variable. Diane was forty-five when she first came to see me and her husband was forty-six. They had two children, Emma, twelve, and Jack, ten.

Diane was the middle child in a family of five closely spaced girls. Her father ran his own small business and her mother was a housewife. She described her family as 'close and caring', but added that they weren't very demonstrative emotionally. She didn't recall ever being hugged by her parents. Diane told me that all five sisters were very feminine and that her parents encouraged them to be 'kind and dutiful'. She added that her parents, although caring towards all of their daughters, rarely treated them as individuals. They generally referred to them as 'the girls', and tended not to single out any of them by name unless that child had been naughty. Diane said she learned very early on to get along and agree with everybody – to 'blend in'. She seemed surprised when I asked her what she especially enjoyed doing as a child and what she'd hoped to do when she grew up. She simply remembered not wanting to be singled out.

Only one of the five, Diane's youngest sister, went to university, and all had married young, except the youngest, who was still single. Diane had met Robert at school – he was in the year ahead of her – and they'd married when she was nineteen. She'd moved straight from the family home to a rented flat with her husband after her marriage.

Diane described her marriage as 'stable but perhaps not exciting'. The couple had hoped to have two children, and both pregnancies were straightforward. She described her daughter Emma as 'shy like her father, rather anxious and keen to please'. Her son Jack was 'much more outgoing, and full of energy'. She was worried that Jack might be difficult as a teenager because, she said, 'he's always testing us'. Other than that, however, the family got on well and were happy together.

Because of Robert's shyness, Diane and he had virtually no social life, although they did visit Diane's parents who lived near by most weekends. Diane also walked dogs at the local dogs' home every Saturday.

Diane told me that because of what she regarded as a restricted social life, her work meant a great deal to her because it provided her with a social outlet. She said she very much enjoyed chatting with colleagues during coffee and lunch breaks. That was why, she added, the panic attacks puzzled her so much. What could make her feel so frightened, when she was so enjoying being part of what she described as 'a warm and friendly group of friends'?

I asked Diane whether she thought there was anything or anyone at work who might be triggering her panicky feelings. She felt certain that there was no pattern; that the attacks occurred 'out of the blue'. I explained that panic attacks almost never occur repeatedly unless there was a reason behind them. In order for us to discover what that might be, I suggested that she keep a record of her attacks for one month: when they occurred, who she was with, where she was and what had been happening during the previous half hour.

When she returned for her next appointment, Diane began by commenting how surprised she'd been to find that she *always* had at least one panic attack every Thursday, and always during the late afternoon. We talked a bit about what happened at that time, and it turned out that Thursday was the day that Emma had a dancing lesson after school, and Diane liked to leave work promptly so she could take her to the lesson.

As it happened, Thursday turned out to be the same day that one of the other secretaries, a woman who was much less organised than Diane, also needed to leave work promptly. This woman regularly approached Diane just before leaving time and asked her to finish bits of work for her. Diane always took on the work without question, but then she was either rushed off her feet or she had to ring Robert and ask him to take Emma to the lesson, knowing Emma would feel neglected.

When I asked her why she always accepted the extra work (the other secretary was, in fact, her junior), she seemed surprised, and after a long pause admitted that she didn't know why. She'd just always assumed that she should help out. When I asked whether colleagues, and this woman in particular, ever did work for her, she replied that she'd 'never put them to such trouble'. We then looked at the circumstances surrounding other panic attacks, and it seemed that all of them were associated either with a request to take on extra (unpaid) work, or else her own worry that someone might be about to make such a request.

It was beginning to look like Diane was shouldering far more responsibility than her job description called for, so for her next homework assignment I asked her to keep track of how much unpaid overtime she was actually doing. She found that it was considerable – about four to six extra hours of unpaid work every week. This wasn't because she was slow or incompetent. On the contrary, she told me that whenever she was appraised, she was always commended and her efficiency was always considered to be far higher than what was expected of her.

I then asked her how often she'd been promoted or given a salary rise. 'Never,' she told me. I wondered if she'd ever asked for a promotion. Again, she seemed surprised, and commented that she didn't know it was appropriate for her to ask for such a thing.

Gradually, Diane began to notice that other secretaries were much more forthright when asked to take on extra work – if it was inconvenient, they were willing to say so. No wonder everyone turned to her, Diane realised. And no wonder she'd begun to dread the late afternoons, when everyone was winding up their work and looking for ways to finish quickly. These were the times when she ignored her own needs and allowed herself to be put upon by others.

The next step was to get Diane to practise saying 'No' if a colleague made a difficult request. I took on the role of the other secretaries, and she had to refuse my requests. At first, Diane felt awkward and nervous, but she soon began to enjoy the role play. She was reminded of how much she'd loved acting as a child, and how she'd immersed herself in the school plays. She'd always loved everything about theatre, particularly dressing up and learning to act in ways that were different from her usual self.

When the time came for her to put our practice to the test, Diane was nervous – 'although I don't feel nearly as anxious as I used to feel when I was asked to do something I knew I couldn't finish in reasonable time,' she told me. She found quite quickly that it was easier than she'd imagined to say 'No' if a request seemed unfair or extremely inconvenient.

By now, Diane was leading our conversations. She told me that she'd been surprised and pleased to discover three consequences of her new assertiveness. First, none of her colleagues shunned her as she'd feared they might – 'In fact,' she said, 'they seem to respect me more.' Second, she found that she enjoyed helping others out when it was convenient, 'far more than I ever did before'. And finally, the panic attacks had all but disappeared and she noticed that she was generally feeling more energetic.

At our final meeting, Diane asked me to help her with one further aspect at work. Her next review at work was coming up soon, and she wanted to practise asking for a promotion. The following week Diane left me a message to say that she'd been promoted and given an extra pay rise.

## What Diane's experience tells us

Diane is an excellent example of a typical middle born. On the one hand, her social and co-operative skills had enabled her to fit well into the workplace and, at the same time, to adapt to a home life with a husband who was less outgoing than she. On the other hand, however, her desire to 'fit in' meant that others had begun to take advantage of her, without Diane even realising it.

Diane used her enjoyment of the theatrical to practise being more assertive in preparation for standing up for herself in the workplace. We took only very small steps so that she could always reassure herself that she wasn't losing the friendships that mattered so much to her at work. In fact, during our last two sessions it was Diane who suggested we take things faster. She'd learned how to listen to herself, and to be more aware not just of how to please and get along with others, but also how to achieve what she wanted from her job.

### CASE STUDY: Peter

Peter was fifty-one when he was referred to me. He'd been suffering for over six months from severe insomnia. After a time, he'd been prescribed sleeping tablets and they'd worked at first, but after about six weeks they were no longer effective. He now spent much of each night tossing and turning, unable to lie still. He told me that he'd begun to dread even trying to go to bed, because he was sure he wouldn't fall asleep. Some nights he was sure he hadn't had any sleep at all.

Peter said that he was no longer able to relax, even on holiday, or to 'switch off' his thoughts, which he described as 'worries that race around in circles and go nowhere'. He'd become so totally exhausted that he was no longer able to get up for work. His GP had signed him off work for six weeks on the understanding that he would seek some therapy.

His problem had begun gradually, not long after he'd been promoted in his job just over a year earlier. He worked in Human Resources (HR) in a large and successful company, and over the years he'd been promoted steadily. It was only last year, when he'd been made head of HR that his problems began.

Life at home was good, Peter said. He'd been married for twenty-six years; he described the relationship as 'solid and supportive'. Lately, however, he'd begun to worry that his wife was getting fed up with his restlessness at night. In fact, on several occasions she'd left in the middle of the night to sleep elsewhere. Although she reassured him that it wasn't important, Peter was worried that his insomnia might also affect his marriage. His wife, Sarah, had always been the homemaker – Peter described her as the rock of the family – and he relied on her steady and cheerful nature to lift his spirits when he felt low. They had two children, both of whom were now at university. Peter told me he was extremely proud of them both, but that he was becoming concerned that if he couldn't continue to work he'd be unable to help support them financially in their studies. Recently, this had become one of his chief worries.

Peter was the middle child in a family of three boys. He described his upbringing as 'completely ordinary . . . unremarkable'. His father worked in a factory and his mother was a housewife. They still lived in the house where he'd grown up, and were in good health and enjoying life. He and his brothers now got on well, although as boys they'd been extremely competitive and had constantly vied with one another. His elder brother was a surveyor and his younger brother, like Peter, worked in HR. Peter admitted that his younger brother had always looked up to him, and had often told Peter that he'd chosen his own career to emulate him. However, he added ruefully, 'Geoff never seems stressed. He never lets his job get to him.'

When they were young, Peter had been the peacemaker. He was the one, he said, who always diffused anger when tempers flared, and when they competed with one another, he was the one who found ways to make the loser feel better. 'That's why', he said, 'HR was such an obvious choice of career for me – sorting things out when there's trouble.'

As we began to examine Peter's childhood in greater detail, it became apparent that his peacemaking efforts had usually come at a cost. The solutions he'd proposed as a child usually meant that he was the one who did the compromising, or that he gave his brothers full credit when he, too, deserved some praise. He began to see that he'd adapted this approach in his work as an adult, and that for many years it had worked well. However, his latest promotion meant that he now had to do more than simply 'smooth the waters'. In the first few months as manager, he'd had to ask two colleagues to resign, and to find four further redundancies. He'd always described his chief asset as 'being someone everybody likes' – but he'd now had to make himself unpopular with some of his colleagues. His promotion, he now understood, had threatened the very foundations of his self-image. It was, he admitted with enormous relief, more responsibility than he wished to shoulder.

It was Peter himself who came up with a possible compromise (of course!). He suggested that he'd ask Sarah if she'd be willing to help him find ways to cut back spending at home. If they found that was possible without threatening their children's places at university, he would then ask if he could be reinstated in his former position at work. To his delight, rather than cutting back their expenditure, Sarah told him that she was keen to find a part-time job herself. She explained that she'd begun to feel restless since their younger daughter had left for university, and she considered this the perfect 'push' she needed to find some work. On the strength of this gesture of positive support, Peter then spoke to his line manager at work. He was told that he was so valued that his request would be honoured, but that his salary would remain at the level of senior manager. Peter was obviously delighted.

He was now sleeping better and feeling much more energetic and positive. We agreed that there was no longer any need to meet.

## What Peter's experience tells us

Peter's skill as a compromiser and negotiator, typical of a middle born, had served him so well that he'd been promoted at work to a level where he felt unhappy. However, when he directed his talents towards solving his own problems, it didn't take him long to find a way out of his difficulties.

Furthermore, this 'setback' made him realise that he'd never really stopped to examine his priorities or to determine whether he was happy about the direction his career was taking. What he now saw was that for him, a 'career path' was relatively unimportant. He was happiest when he was able to work comfortably, rather than to push past his limits, and he now recognised that promotions and higher salaries were not as important to him as satisfaction at work.

## Middle Borns in a Nutshell

To sum up, here are the characteristics most often associated with a middle born:

- Good social skills – aware of and sensitive to the needs of others and adept at finding compromises

- Easily swayed by the opinions of others

- Realistic about the extent of their abilities, but often without a clear vision of what they most want in life

- Likely to fight for the underprivileged and needy, but less likely to ask for help for themselves when distressed

- Prone to phases of dressing and otherwise presenting themselves in an unusual or extreme manner, particularly when younger

- Likely to excel in non-academic ways

- Liable to leave home at a younger age than their siblings

It's time now to turn to the youngest member of the family.

# Chapter Three

# Last Borns

This is the birth-order position that people most often say they'd choose. As the youngest person in the family you're always the 'baby', the one everyone else loves to look after. Any mistakes or inadequacies tend to be excused, when you ask for help you usually get it and no one's constantly nagging you to 'grow up and do it yourself'. When other family members act in an immature way they're usually either ignored or frowned upon, but when you behave in exactly the same way you're likely to be pandered to, fussed over and indulged – and more often than not, you get the help you were seeking.

Why is there such a big difference in attitude towards the last born as compared to the others in the family? After all, we were all cute babies once. Why are children in other birth positions either ignored or urged to 'grow up' and figure things out for themselves? To answer these questions, we need to turn once again to the family and examine the environment in which the last born grows up.

## Your Family Environment

A number of medical and social advances over the last fifty years have changed our attitudes to raising a family profoundly, and the effects of this revolution have made a particularly strong impact on last borns. Breakthroughs in our understanding of human reproduction mean that we now have a great deal of control over whether and when we have children. That means, in turn, that parents are able to decide with reasonable confidence how many children they wish to have and are therefore fully aware that when they have their last-born child, it is likely to be the last time they'll fulfil their role as parents.

Although this awareness is no doubt accompanied by a sense of relief for many parents, it also brings with it feelings of nostalgia and regret. For your parents, you were the last baby they would raise: each of your 'first' milestones was a 'last time' for them. Often – without any awareness of what they were doing – it meant that your parents rewarded you when you showed dependent and immature behaviours. Parents do this because they're not yet ready to give up their parenting role – one that we often tend to idealise when we're about to lose it. Note, for example, how we talk with sympathy about those who are suffering from the 'empty-nest syndrome'.

At the same time, parents often overprotect and/or spoil their last born. Some will even freely admit that they tried *too* hard when raising their youngest and that in particular they were overly indulgent, as if to make amends for any mistakes they felt they'd made when raising their older children.

None the less, your parents were also more experienced parents. By the time you came along they would have had a pretty good idea of what was worth bothering about and what misbehaviours could be ignored. Furthermore, they probably had less time to check on and discipline you – less at any rate than they had for your older brothers and sisters. That's why people often say that they envied their youngest sibling – it looks like the youngest got away with so much more than they did.

Another difference is that there were more family members on hand to help you out whenever you asked – more so than there were for any other of the children. That means you who are youngest in your family probably never had to struggle with a problem for very long on your own.

Finally, no new brother or sister ever came along to take away your role as 'the baby of the family'. That means you never really had any reason to give up any dependent, childish ways you might have had.

Thus, you last borns grew up in an atmosphere that encouraged you to remain dependent and to expect to be taken care of and indulged. In effect, that atmosphere encourages more charm than effort!

## Typical Characteristics of a Last Born

Let's take a look in detail now at the characteristics that are most likely to develop in the atmosphere described above:

### Last borns have an outgoing, charming and 'cute' nature – they're often the entertainers when they're with other people

You last borns tend to be sociable creatures, and, moreover, enjoy being the centre of attention. You're very often regarded as the focus of the group, and/or the clown – the one who entertains everyone and makes them laugh.

It's easy to understand why this pattern of behaviour becomes habitual. Remember, there will already have been at least one other child in the family – perhaps more – and they'll have been more mature and more skilled and experienced than those of you who are the youngest. The others gained parental attention for being more grown-up and for showing how well they could learn new skills. With respect to Darwin's Principle of Divergence (see page 36), that means that if you're the youngest in your family, you had to find a new way to behave, one that was different from your older siblings', but that also made you at least as attractive as them. In particular, if your parents were acutely aware that it was 'the last time round' with you – it probably meant you received lots of extra attention whenever you behaved in 'cute' and baby-like ways. Your parents considered your babyish qualities to be endearing, instead of simply something they had to put up with until you finally managed to grow up a bit more.

Plus, because no baby came along after you – one who'd, of course, be much better at behaving in a charmingly helpless manner – your dependent behaviour pattern was never threatened. You never had a compelling reason to give up your attention-seeking antics and develop new and more mature ways of behaving. In effect, those of you who are last born had every reason to continue cultivating child-like characteristics for as long as possible.

This may not, however, always serve you well. Whereas dependent, helpless behaviour in a child is considered cute or endearing, in an adult it may carry less pleasant connotations. This takes us to the second characteristic of last borns:

## Last borns can be manipulative

In its extreme form, charm becomes manipulation. At that point it's no longer attractive because it causes everyone who's around the manipulator to feel overwhelmed and trapped, particularly when they feel that too much is being demanded of them. As with so many human interactions, whether as a last born you merely continue to behave in a helpless manner, or instead you start to become quite manipulative, depends on how others respond to your behaviour.

If when you were charming and apparently needy as a

child you were appreciated and humoured, you're unlikely ever to change your behaviour. If you were instead encouraged to do things for yourself, and were shown how to do so and then praised for trying, you no doubt became less needy and demanding as you grew older. Too often, however, parents deal with their last born in a confusing, ambivalent manner. They want their youngest to be baby-like and sweet and yet not too much of a bother. This confusing message often causes the youngest child to progress from behaving in a pleasantly attention-seeking way to becoming frustrated and manipulative.

The effect of parental ambivalence is examined in Chapter Five. Suffice it for now to say that ambivalence towards a last born is most likely to strengthen and deepen an anxious dependence in them, rather than to encourage them either to become more independent and mature or simply to 'turn on the charm'.

## Last borns are often rather disorganised, but at the same time they're comfortable with this tendency

Because you last borns focus so much of your attention on what others can do for you, it means that there's less time available for setting goals for yourself and organising your own behaviour (or planning for and organising that of others, as would a first born). Furthermore, because you've probably come to expect others to sort you out, you may never take the time to stop periodically and think about what you're doing and where you're going – again, as would a first born. That means you quite often appear undirected or even chaotic.

This lack of organisation and direction probably bothers you less than it will the people around you – in particular anxious, goal-directed first borns and singles. None the less, it's actually not a bad thing. The attitude has its drawbacks, but it also has a positive side, as we shall see in the next section.

## Last borns are often creative and innovative

Although on the one hand disorganisation is associated with a lack of predetermination, it's also linked with creativity. Carefully constructed plans cause us to ignore fresh possibilities – without such plans we're able to remain open to new and different ways of thinking about what's going on around us.

It's a fact that many of our greatest innovators and groundbreakers have been last borns, or at least the youngest son or daughter in a family. The American psychologist Frank Sulloway examined the lives and, in particular, the birth-order positions of a number of creative and innovative people. He used Darwin's Principle of Divergence (see page 36) to explain why he believes that these last borns were driven to find new ways of looking at the world.

The problem you last borns face is that you haven't as many ways open to you when it comes to attracting parental attention because older siblings have already become competent in most, if not all, of the more conventional ones. That leaves you with no choice but to break new ground in order to be noticed. Sulloway describes the backgrounds of a vast number of innovators to prove his point. He even cites Charles Darwin himself as an example of this principle – Darwin was the fifth of six children, the youngest son in his family.

## Last borns tend to be rebellious, and more likely than others to challenge authority

If you're breaking new ground, you are 'rebelling' against the conventional, and your behaviour will be interpreted by many as a challenge to authority and to the more traditional, established ways of behaving.

A respect for authority (first-born behaviour) and a tendency to compromise in order to ease social friction (middle-born behaviour) are great attributes if what you want to do is to maintain the status quo. However, if you're going to stand any chance of making a creative breakthrough, it's necessary to reject and set aside established rules and methods, as well as all the usual ways of looking at what's going on. Because last borns are compelled to find a different way to gain attention, they're the ones who are most likely to turn convention on its head in this way. These last borns are almost always considered rebels during their lifetime – and ground-breakers, even geniuses, only much later on.

Of course, it's a great deal easier for you last borns to get away with breaking rules and behaving in unconventional ways than it is for the older siblings in the family. Your parents would have been more experienced and busier than they were when they had fewer children, and more liable to indulge their last born than they were the others.

## Last borns are more likely than others to take risks

This characteristic goes hand in hand with the tendency to challenge authority figures and the existing rules and regulations they promote. You last borns, remember, are looking for ways to differentiate yourself from your older siblings, and with most of the safer, more conventional routes already taken by the older ones, you're left with riskier options.

It's in children's nature to push against and test the limits that have been set for them, and this, coupled with the fact that parents tend to relax the boundaries with each successive child, means that the last born is pushing against the widest limits – and therefore seeking out the riskiest options.

So it's logical to assume that you last borns were more likely to take risks as children, because you had to compete with your older siblings – and therefore try harder and engage in less conventional or simple ways of accessing the things you wanted. But does this risk-taking behaviour persist once you've grown up and moved away from sibling competition? A recent study of baseball players by Frank Sulloway and his colleague, Richard Zweigenhaft, suggests that it does.

Sulloway and Zweigenhaft looked at 'base stealing' in the game of baseball. This is when if you manage to steal the base – that is, run from one point of safety to the next before you're spotted – you'll come closer to scoring a point for your team. It's regarded as a high-risk strategy, however, because if you're caught you lose your chance of scoring at all at that point in the game. Sulloway and Zweigenhaft found that younger brothers were 10.6 times more likely to try to steal a base than were older siblings – and, of course, because they tried to do so relatively more often than the older siblings, they were more practised and therefore more successful at doing so.

Thus far, we've painted a fairly enviable picture of life for those of you who are the youngest in your family. You were parented by experienced adults who probably indulged and pampered you, but who also allowed you relative freedom to do and think what you liked.

Apart from a tendency to become manipulative, are there, therefore, *any* disagreeable characteristics associated with this birth-order position? Yes, I think there are two:

## Last borns are vulnerable to low self-esteem and to feelings of inferiority

This characteristic makes sense if you look at life from a last born's point of view. Everyone around you is bigger, stronger and more competent than you. You may even have seen yourself as 'behind' from the start. Of course, first borns often view themselves in this way as well, but they see fewer individuals around them, and – at least at first – most of the people they see are fully grown adults who are caring for them, rather than other children who are competing with them. You're less liable to compare yourself to your caregivers – you may try to emulate them instead – whereas it's natural to measure yourself against your competitors (namely your older siblings). The problem for last borns is that when you make your comparisons, you're liable to conclude that you're less competent than others. Yet this is through no fault of your own; it's simply because the others have had a head start on life. None the less, this observation may cause you to feel even more helpless than you might have done because what gives your older siblings their advantage – their age and experience – is something you can't change or control in any way.

Because you're more likely than others to feel inferior – or at least less competent than others – you're also in danger of concluding that it's not worth trying to do things for yourself. This then reinforces your tendency to remain dependent on everyone else. This vicious circle may fuel any low opinion you may create with regard to your own capabilities.

A recent and – in my opinion – misguided approach to parenting is another reason why some last borns, particularly those who've grown up in recent years, have a tendency to doubt their capabilities. In the 1980s and '90s there was a great deal of talk about how important it is to 'nourish your children's self-esteem' by telling them how wonderful and fantastic they are, whether or not they've actually earned that praise. Studies, in particular those spear-headed by Professor Carol Dweck at Columbia University in New York, have, however, shown that this approach can be counterproductive. A belief in one's abilities, as well as high self-esteem, are more readily found in children who are praised for their efforts, rather than for some static quality – in other words, for how hard they try, rather than for what they achieve. So, for example, there's more chance that a child will develop high self-esteem and dare to take on difficult challenges if they're told that they 'try really hard' than if they're told that they are 'clever'.

Of course, all children are vulnerable to the pitfalls of this misguided approach to parenting. However, in my experience it is you last borns who are most at risk. This is in part because your parents tended to dote on you more, and therefore to heap praise on you with little regard to its validity. It's also because the people you saw around you probably appeared to be so much 'smarter' or more 'brilliant' than you were, so it was easy to doubt the sincerity of what others said to you. Such dispiriting evidence may have led you to doubt not only yourself, but also any praise that came your way.

## Last borns are easily disappointed and prone to feeling 'let down' by others

The more often someone is catered to and the longer they're taken care of rather than encouraged to care for themselves, the higher the chance that they'll feel let down by others in later life. This is a danger that particularly affects last borns. You grew up with an expectation that other people – particularly parental figures – will automatically 'know' what you want and that they'll generally be keen to provide it for you.

Now that may indeed have been the case when you were a precious little child. However, when you grew older and began to mix with peers you may have been surprised – even hurt – to discover that they expected a more even-handed relationship. Thus, you are left feeling disappointed and let down by others, wondering if they really care about you at all. A dangerous consequence of this sort of attitude is that you may start blaming everyone else when things don't go your way. By failing to take responsibility in this way, you lose the opportunity to improve your circumstances.

This illustrates once again how parental styles and attitudes are inextricably bound up with birth position itself – how, that is, they work together to create the 'typical' characteristics we find associated with each birth-order position. We'll examine this and other interactions later on. For now, simply keep in mind that everything in these birth-order profiles will mean much more, and make more sense, once you've woven in the qualifying factors you'll be reading about in Part Two.

## The Last Born's Guide to Choosing a Partner

The happiest choice of partner for most last borns is a first born, someone who will organise them and consider it natural to look after and take care of them. The last born's rebelliousness will, in turn, delight many rule-abiding first borns – that is, they can enjoy vicariously the risk-taking behaviour of a last-born partner without having to fly in the face of conventional wisdom themselves.

However, there is a potential problem with this last born/first born combination. Last borns who are stubbornly passionate about their own beliefs may clash with a conventional first born if that first born insists on setting all the house rules.

Another good match for a last born is a middle born. The middle born – amenable and willing to compromise – is more likely than anyone else to allow a last born to pursue their dreams, however unconventional or unworkable these might seem. There may be less order and not as much goal-directed behaviour in this pairing as there would be with a last born and a first born, but the relationship has more chance of being an amicable one.

Last borns who choose another last born are likely to form an extremely creative partnership, and one that others will be drawn to because it will appear to be so interesting and so dynamic. On the other hand, two last borns may find it difficult to plan ahead sensibly and to ensure that the mundane tasks of daily life are completed. Life for two last borns may, in other words, be rather chaotic!

Last borns and singles can make a good match. Singles, who are generally sensible and conscientious, can take charge of their less-organised partner. They, in turn, will benefit from the last born who will introduce a sense of creativity and adventure into the relationship.

## The Last Born's Guide to Choosing a Career

The ideal career for you is one where you can work at your own pace, with the freedom to pursue and develop ideas as they occur to you. Creative fields – design, invention and innovation – are best. However, for most of us that amount of freedom is rarely given at the outset of our working lives. We must earn it by first working to the requirements and timetables of others; and last borns, more than other individuals, will need to have that initial organisation and scheduling imposed on them in no uncertain terms. At the same time, you'll be happiest if your superiors impose these guidelines in such a way that you imagine you have more freedom than you actually do. This subtle approach is the best way to encourage creativity and original thinking in a last born.

If you choose to work alone and/or for yourself – and many last borns do – you'll have to learn how to be self-disciplined. This is certainly possible, but it's likely to be harder for you than it will be for many other people.

> ## *Famous last borns*
>
> - Janet Jackson
>
> - Johnny Depp
>
> - Joan of Arc
>
> - Eddie Murphy

## CASE STUDY: Louise

'I'm not going to get my hopes up this time. I won't expect you to sort me out – no one else ever has done. Why should this time be any different?'

This was how Louise began our first session together. She was twenty-eight years old and had been referred by her GP for what he'd described as a 'depression with symptoms of anxiety'. She'd made an appointment to see him because she hadn't been able to sleep for several weeks and was now, as she put it, 'losing it' at work because she was too tired to concentrate. He'd put her on a low dose of antidepressants and suggested she have some psychotherapy.

Louise had been working for four years as an events organiser in a small theatre. She arranged fund raising and planned for schools to visit the theatre and attend special performances. She told me that she enjoyed her work (it was the longest period of time she'd stayed in the same job) but that she wished really she could be onstage herself – 'If only I was good enough.'

She'd been renting a flat with her partner of three years until the relationship had broken down four months earlier. Richard, a management consultant, was her third serious boyfriend. 'However,' Louise told me, 'like the others, he let me down once the honeymoon period wore off.' After moving in with her parents for a few weeks, just after the break-up, she'd found a small flat near her work and was living there on her own. She said she missed the comfort of a relationship, but felt it was right that they'd split up. 'Richard was always complaining that I was too demanding of him,' she commented, 'but I think he's the one who was too demanding. For example, he used to complain that I'd leave everything in a mess in the flat – it drove him crazy that I never got around to sorting things out.'

When they first got together Louise told me that she'd loved the way Richard liked to look after her. But things changed when they'd moved in together last year. 'That's when he began to seem more like a control freak than just someone strong and caring. And I realised we hardly shared any interests – he didn't like to have fun like I do, so I was out with friends more and more, while he just stayed home and watched TV. I think we both knew things were ending between us.'

She told me that she had a group of friends who were strongly supportive. They were a diverse lot – most of them she'd met through work, although one had been her friend since they were in drama school together. She said that she talked to or texted her friends most days, went to the gym with one of them several times a week, and met up with some of the others frequently for drinks or lunch. Her friends were always telling her what fun she was to be with, even after the break-up, but Louise felt they were only trying to humour her. 'It always feels like I'm working so hard to be funny and make everyone laugh,' she added, 'when I just wish sometimes I could relax a bit.'

Louise had started feeling restless and anxious shortly after she'd moved into her own flat. With no one around at night to encourage her to keep a routine, she said, 'I rather lost a sense of schedule. I was eating at any time, anywhere, and not getting into bed until really late. Then when I'd finally get into bed, I'd start to worry and it would take ages to get to sleep. Getting up in time for work was becoming more and more difficult.' When I asked her what she was worrying about, she replied, 'It just seems like my life is going nowhere. Everybody else seems to have plans, but not me.'

Louise had grown up not far from where she was living now, the youngest of four children. Her brothers were in their thirties, married with children, and had good jobs. She described both as 'responsible and caring – they were always so good to Sarah and me. But I wouldn't want to live their lives. It seems too boring!' Sarah, thirty-one, was a primary school teacher like her mother. She lived with her boyfriend who was also a teacher. Louise said they were hoping to start a family soon.

Her parents had been married for forty years, and Louise described the marriage as 'content, I think'. She said her parents never seemed to argue, but that 'they never seem to talk that much about anything important, either. They just get on, I suppose.' Her mother had taught at a secondary school until she'd become pregnant with her first child. Louise said she suspected she'd always wanted a big family, and that she enjoyed her role as mother and housewife.

Her father, a solicitor, she described as 'kind but rather distant. He's a routines sort of person – everything has to be in order.' She added that her parents had been quite strict with the boys, but easier with Sarah, and 'probably too easy with me'.

Louise described her childhood as 'unremarkable'. As a teenager, she admitted she was 'pretty wild'. She drank and smoked a lot, although she didn't think her parents were particularly aware of her habits. Sam, the youngest of her two brothers had behaved similarly, and after a number of rows with his parents had left home at sixteen. 'That made me very careful,' she said. 'I hated all those arguments, and I didn't want to feel like I'd have to leave home so young, like Sam. I wasn't ready.'

Louise said she was 'just an average student, and I didn't ever work very hard'. At her parents' insistence she studied English and drama at A level, 'just so I could be looked after at home for a bit longer'. Her parents wanted her to go to university, but she insisted on trying to get into drama school instead. 'I know my parents were disappointed, but at the time I didn't care. I just wanted to get into acting.' She was accepted into one of the drama schools she'd applied to and started with high hopes, but dropped out after a year. 'It was too much like hard work,' she commented.

Since that time, Louise had worked in a number of jobs, most of them related to drama or theatre in some way. She told me that she was easily bored – 'the jobs always turn out to be more tedious than they seemed at first' – although, much to her own delight and surprise, she was still enjoying her present work after more than four years. When I asked her what had held her interest, she said that it was probably because she was given so much freedom to come up with ideas herself. She had two assistants who then helped her turn those ideas into reality.

I asked Louise what she most hoped to achieve in therapy, and she seemed surprised. 'Aren't you supposed to tell *me*?' she asked. 'I had some counselling at drama school, and again after I broke up with my first boyfriend, and those therapists told *me* what I needed to work on. Isn't that what I need, to be told?' When I suggested that she might feel more motivated to work hard in therapy if she set the goals herself, she said she agreed that there was some sense in that. She therefore set as her first goal for herself, to learn how to sleep better and feel more rested. Her second goal, she decided, was to get back to work (she'd been signed off by her GP for a month). Her third was to 'get clearer about what I really want out of life'.

It didn't take Louise long to establish good sleep habits, and she was delighted when she felt rested enough to return to work – her second goal – within a fortnight. Her third aim, to find some clear direction, proved more difficult, however. It took some time for her to recognise the pattern of dependency she'd established, both in her relationships and in her work. She began to see that she always let others do the planning and goal setting. Then, after a time, when that way of life or those plans or whatever didn't suit her well, she'd blame her boyfriend or her job for her dissatisfaction instead of taking responsibility and looking for ways to improve things herself.

At that point it became clear to Louise why she loved her current job so much, and why it continually challenged and interested her. Perhaps more by luck than by design, for the first time in her life she'd found herself in a position where she'd been forced to chart the way ahead, and she'd discovered that actually she loved the planning and goal setting. This realisation encouraged her greatly, and she began to talk in much more specific terms about how she could develop her job even further. She also came to see that although she did want a career that involved theatre, actually she preferred backstage organising to acting itself. 'Always before, whenever I said I was studying drama, everyone assumed I meant acting. So I assumed it, too! I was letting everyone else think *for* me!'

## What Louise's experience tells us

During her time in therapy, Louise learned to use her last-born qualities, in particular her outgoing nature and her willingness to take a risk and try new things, to her advantage. By the time we'd finished working together, she told me that her 'usual sense of fun' was returning, and that she was feeling more adventurous again. Although she said she definitely wasn't yet ready for a 'full-on relationship', she'd also begun to date new people. Now, she said, instead of simply thinking about how someone could meet her own needs, she was thinking about what she, too, could contribute to the relationship, and whether there was any potential to develop new interests with whoever she was with. She told me how good it was to feel 'equal, like a partner instead of a little kid. At last, I feel like I'm growing up and I can see my way ahead.' In effect, Louise no longer needed to be needy – she was enjoying life as an equal with other adults. She'd retained several of the positive qualities of a last born (her sociability and her creativity, for example), but had also learned to take responsibility and had left behind her dependency on others to sort things out for her.

## CASE STUDY: **Steve**

It wasn't the car crash itself that caused Steve to seek therapy. He'd suffered from post-traumatic stress disorder (PTSD) just after the head-on collision that had killed his colleague who'd been driving the car and left him with severe concussion and two broken legs. After the operations on his legs, he'd been treated for the PTSD, and he no longer suffered flashbacks or woke from terrible nightmares.

The reason Steve came to see me was that despite the fact that he appeared to have recovered both physically and mentally from this terrible accident, and had been back at work successfully for two months, he was still feeling anxious and depressed. In fact, he felt so low that he'd begun to consider taking his life. His distress was compounded whenever he thought about his colleague who'd died – Steve felt he should only be grateful that he was still alive. Furthermore, these suicidal thoughts frightened him because he knew they were irrational; most of the time he knew he didn't really want to die.

Steve told me that the reason he felt so hopeless and despondent was the chronic back pain he'd been left with since the accident. The pattern seemed totally random – he'd have several good days and then he'd wake in agony. He worked as a chef, so he was on his feet and active much of the day, and on bad days, he said he could barely complete his shift. His GP had referred him to a number of specialists including a pain-management consultant, but no one could find the cause. He felt let down and helpless. His GP had prescribed antidepressants, and these had reduced his anxiety and made him feel less suicidal. None the less, he knew he was still depressed.

Steve was the youngest of three children. He had two sisters, six and eight years older than him. Steve hadn't been a planned baby, but his parents were delighted when they learned they were going to have a third child, and even more delighted when they discovered that it was to be a much longed-for son. He'd grown up being spoiled and cosseted by his parents, and pampered by his older sisters.

He'd decided early on that he wanted to be a chef. At first, his parents weren't keen – both they and his two sisters had gone to university. However, as usual he was allowed to do what he wished, and had gone to a local college to train. In fact, he proved to have quite a talent for cooking and he did extremely well at college. He was offered a number of jobs initially, and although he moved often from job to job (he was thirty-eight at the time of the accident), he had never been out of work. He was recognised and respected by colleagues, both for his talent and his willingness to work hard.

Steve had had a number of girlfriends. His longest relationship – the one he was in when he came to see me – had lasted four years. He described his girlfriend, Amanda, as 'totally supportive' throughout the accident and during his long process of recovery. Amanda worked full time in banking. They had no children and no plans to start a family.

Steve chose two goals during our work together. He wanted to find a pattern to his pain, so that he could feel life was a bit more predictable, and he wanted to find some strategies for coping with the pain when it hit him. We began our work by devising a diary in which he could record not only the circumstances during painful episodes, but also those when he was feeling particularly well. He was surprised, but on reflection also pleased, to be asked to think about good times as well as painful moments. His depression had meant he'd been in the habit of dwelling only on the pain.

It was clear that Steve expected me to create the pain diary for him, and when I insisted that he choose the variables to record, he became petulant. 'I thought you were supposed to sort me out,' he complained. This was his reaction to a number of discussions about the expectations he had that other people were 'supposed' to take care of him. He'd not realised how reliant he was on others, in particular on women, to make life comfortable for him. At the same time, he acknowledged his ability to work hard, and since the accident, to work through pain. It wasn't long before he began to enjoy devising his diaries, and to feel a growing pride in being able to withstand discomfort. His pain diary suggested a number of ways to make a bout of pain less likely, which increased further his sense of control.

Alongside working to predict his pain episodes more accurately, I suggested that Steve enrol in a mindfulness course at the local pain clinic to help him bear the pain when it did strike. He told me that he found the techniques suggested during this course to be incredibly helpful.

By the end of ten sessions, Steve told me that he was feeling much calmer and happier. He was coping much more effectively with the bouts of pain, and he felt better able to predict when they might strike. From what he'd learned in his diary about the times when he felt best rather than worst, Steve had formulated a number of ways to make it less likely he'd be in pain, and indeed the bouts of pain had become less frequent. He said he was coping well at work and enjoying his time in the kitchen once again. He also reported that things were even better in his relationship; Amanda had told him that he seemed much more willing to accommodate her rather than to expect to be accommodated himself. He said he hadn't realised how selfish he'd become, and that he was pleased he was now aware of this tendency. He added that he had not appreciated how gratifying it could be to please others rather than always expecting to be cared for.

## What Steve's experience tells us

Steve was in many ways a typical last born. He had always expected a great deal from others, and he felt let down by them quite easily. What he learned from his terrible accident was that he was, in fact, able to take care of himself, and he felt a growing self-pride the more he did so. He also learned to use one of the strengths of a last born – his creativity and ability to be innovative – to devise ways to predict and control his pain.

## Last Borns in a Nutshell

To sum up, here are the characteristics that are most typical of the last born in the family:

- Charming and outgoing, the one who most wants to take centre stage in social situations

- Harbouring a tendency to be manipulative

- Oftentimes disorganised and less goal-orientated than others

- Creative and innovative; more likely to go their own way than to accept established views

- Rebellious and ready to challenge authority

- Risk-takers

- Vulnerable to feelings of low self-esteem, self-doubt and inferiority

- Likely to feel easily disappointed in or let down by other people

Next, we'll be looking at the last of the four main birth-order positions: singles.

## Chapter Four

# Single Children

Of all birth-order positions, that of the single child (I prefer this term to 'only' child) has undergone the greatest transformation.

Once upon a time it was unusual, and in some communities it was even considered unacceptable, to choose to have only one child. Singles were thought of as misfits, odd or eccentric, and they were often teased or bullied.

Nowadays, however, it's quite a different story. Things have changed a great deal for those of you who are singles – for the better. To find out why, we need to take a look at how our society has moved on, not only in terms of the way we conceptualise the modern family, but also with regard to the increased freedom that women have in today's society.

Women today have greater control over when they'll have children and how many they'd like to have, much more so than at any time in history. They're able to regard motherhood as a choice, as one aspect of their adult life, rather than as the controlling force that directs all their other plans and dreams. As a result, a significant number of women are choosing to have fewer children so that they can continue to have time for (and to afford comfortably) other interests in addition to becoming a parent.

Because one-child families are increasingly common, it's meant that a number of the negative qualities associated with being the only child in a family – in particular, feeling awkward when trying to socialise with peers and feeling lonely and misunderstood generally – no longer inevitably go hand in hand with being single. Once again, you can see how so many of the characteristics attributed to a particular birth-order position are influenced by the opinions at the time, in addition to anything intrinsic to the individuals they describe. In this case, the negative picture that was painted of singles had more to do with general attitudes and beliefs than with the actual birth position *per se*.

## Your Family Environment

The fact that small families have become more common is by no means the only reason why those of you who are young adult singles today are generally happier and better adjusted than your predecessors. Another critical reason is that your parents are likely to have *chosen* to have one child instead of having only one because it was impossible for them to have any more. That means that your parents would have been happier and more contented, and that you, therefore, grew up in a much healthier atmosphere, around more positive role models.

Furthermore, parents these days are generally more aware of the needs of a growing child, and in particular of how important it is that their offspring learns good social skills. As a result, most go to great lengths to ensure that their child spends time with other children who are similar in age. Consequently, terms such as 'lonely' and 'socially isolated' no longer apply to most singles.

What, then, are the modern descriptors for this birth-order position? What qualities best describe those of you who grew up without siblings?

## *The context is crucial*

Before you begin trying to guess a single's – or anyone's – characteristics, it's important to think about *why* their family is constituted as it is; so, for the purposes of this discussion, *why* a single is the only child in that family.

If, for example, a single's parents desperately wanted to have a large family, and if perhaps they also had difficulty conceiving at all, then they're likely to have raised the one child they did have to be over-protected, demanding, anxious and spoiled. In those circumstances, the single's character will most closely resemble that of a last born whose parents didn't wish to 'lose' their baby (see page 54). And, in both cases, that individual is most likely to be described as an unhappy, perpetually dissatisfied and demanding person, who always expects others to do everything for them.

Consider, on the other hand, a single born to parents who'd either decided in the first place to have only the one child, or who, once they realised that this was the only one they would have, chose to be pleased with their new circumstances. Under these conditions, the individual they raise will almost certainly adopt the most positive characteristics typical of his birth position (see below).

This is why it is crucial to look at context when considering the characteristics of a person in this (or indeed any) birth-order position.

## Typical Characteristics of a Single

These are the characteristics that most often distinguish a single:

### Singles are extremely articulate and likely to be academically successful

Those of you who are singles, like first borns, tend to do well in school, both because you're able to express yourselves clearly and well and because you're used to and skilled at interacting with adults. After all, those in both of these birth-order positions enjoyed a period of time in their early development when they received the exclusive attention of their parents and, therefore, all the rich linguistic input that goes with child–adult exchanges.

The difference, however, is that you never had to lose that exclusivity, nor did you have to learn how to share parental care and attention. Instead, you continued to enjoy these privileges throughout the whole of your schooling. That means you didn't suffer from anxious, jealous feelings that can interfere with attention and memory as you absorbed what your parents had to teach you.

Therefore, not only did you have the best conditions in which to learn and to retain rich and well-developed communication skills, you were also able to enjoy them indefinitely.

### Singles tend to have high levels of self-confidence

Barring any destabilising event such as parental separation or the loss of a parent, singles are unlikely to lose the fond and exclusive attention of either parent. Quite the contrary, you're very often showered more or less continuously with love and approval. When parents decide that they'll only have one child, they're very likely to direct a great deal of their energies towards them. You benefited richly, because when individuals are sure they're loved and when they receive positive attention whenever they need it, their self-confidence develops healthily.

Of course, there's potential in this situation for things to go wrong, just as in the same way it can go wrong for last borns. If parents shower undeserved praise on their child, or if they forget to praise their child's efforts more highly than they do their achievements (see pages 61–2), then that child may begin to feel pressured, overprotected or, worst of all, to doubt either their own capabilities or their parents' sincerity. Also, if parents shower too much attention on a child, that child may feel overprotected and trapped, as though they are living their lives for their parents rather than for themselves Thankfully, however – at least in my own clinical experience – most parents of singles seem to get the balance right and raise confident, assertive individuals.

## Singles show a preference for and an identification with others who are older

You've grown up in a world of adults at home, so it will feel natural for you to seek out the company and the approval of those who are older and more mature than you are. After all, that's what you're used to doing.

First borns are also likely to affiliate with older individuals. However, there is a difference in the motivation behind this affiliation. First borns and singles alike seek out authority figures because they both wish to gain their praise and approval. For first borns, however, this is by far the most powerful reason for their preference. You singles, on the other hand, tend to be less hungry for approval. After all, you probably had plenty of it when you were growing up. You seek out older company primarily because you feel most comfortable around those who are older.

## Singles are able to amuse themselves happily and to spend significant amounts of time alone

This is perhaps unsurprising, but it's none the less worth mentioning because it distinguishes singles from those in other birth-order positions. Of course, there will be some first borns, middles and last borns who also enjoy spending time on their own – these are the introverts, as you'll learn in Chapter Nine. Proportionately, however, there will be fewer of them.

Furthermore, you're not only used to being on your own, you're also quite likely to enjoy spending time in that way. You're less prone than others to feel anxious if no one else is around, and you express feelings of loneliness less often. You're used to coming up with your own amusements and finding ways to entertain yourselves, much more so than those who had brothers and sisters around to offer them constant entertainment and ready-made diversions.

## Singles have a logical and organised mindset

Adults, just like children, experience and understand the world both through their understanding (logic) and their feelings (emotions). The difference, however, is that adults, unlike children, regularly find themselves in situations where they're meant to behave more or less entirely logically. Therefore, most adults have learned how to repress their emotional side, and also to recognise ahead of time when it's advisable to do so.

Because you singles grew up primarily around adults, you'll be more used to expecting a logical transaction when you interact with other people. You never had to put up with siblings who threw tantrums, nor were you regularly forced to abandon logic to argue jealously with them. Without these competitive others around to stir up emotions, you had little need to abandon a logical approach to get what you wanted. Your sensible, unemotional problem-solving skills are likely, therefore, to predominate and develop powerfully.

You're probably also good at planning ahead, at making lists and at organising yourself. As a result, you're very often considered to be 'the reliable one' when you meet up with others for group activities, and therefore – like first borns – are often asked to take on positions of responsibility. These opportunities, in turn, allow you to improve your planning and organisational skills still further.

There's another interesting comparison that can be made between singles and first borns. Both tend to behave responsibly and reliably, most likely because they've so often observed and then copied that sort of behaviour from the adults they grew up with. However, as we know, the first born behaves in this way primarily to gain approval from others. Singles seek such approval as well, but not to the same extent – no doubt because you never lost your parents' focus to a new sibling and therefore never knew what it's like to feel desperate to regain it. For you, responsible, reliable behaviour is simply a habit.

Thus far, the more modern single appears to be in quite a fortunate position. What a stellar list of attributes! Once considered the least desirable birth-order position, that of the single now (at least in my opinion) is one of the two most enviable (the other being that of the last born). You received plenty of adult care and attention and were never threatened with losing it. As a result, you probably did very well academically, you're likely to be self-confident and you're happy to spend time alone. Furthermore, there's less chance of you suffering from feelings of anxiety and jealousy than those who grew up in larger families.

Are there, then, any negative aspects of growing up as a single? Yes, I believe that there are three less desirable qualities that can be attributed to this birth-order position:

## Singles are prone to unease or discomfort when socialising with peers, often feeling 'misunderstood'

Although parents of singles usually make enormous efforts to provide their child with plenty of opportunities to socialise with their peers, these interactions will be fairly circumscribed. They're likely to have been planned, time-limited and supervised by adults – certainly, at least, when you were younger. That means you'll have missed out on learning the skills needed to establish 'territory' without an adult there to sort things out for you, to stand up for yourself diplomatically and find ways to share limited toys and space.

Those children who grow up with brothers and sisters have to learn to think fast, to read other people's desires and intended actions (and to take advantage of that knowledge) and stand up for what they believe to be right or what they feel they deserve – without the help of adults. Singles miss out, often entirely, but certainly in terms of sheer frequency, on such opportunities to develop 'street smart' skills. This means you're more likely than others to behave in ways that lead to misunderstandings. Even when this doesn't actually happen, singles often tell me that they feel distanced from their peers and awkward when they try to join in group activities.

## Singles show a strong tendency to perfectionism

Being practical and sensible and wanting to do everything as expertly as possible is all very well. However, it's also important to know how and when to relax and let things slide a little. Without this counterbalance, we are prone to burnout and other disorders that result when the pressure is unrelenting.

When we're growing up it's natural for us to compare ourselves to those around us. Given that there's usually a preponderance of admiring and encouraging adults in the single's life – throughout childhood – it means that they set their standards in relation to them. That means you'll almost certainly shoot high and expect a great deal of yourself.

## Singles find it difficult to tolerate disorder

In larger families someone's always knocking over someone else's carefully arranged set of blocks or deleting their favourite game on the computer, so individuals in those families have plenty of opportunities to figure out what to do when things go wrong. That wasn't the case for you singles. When things in your life fell into disarray, there was usually an adult on hand to sort it out, more or less straight away. That means you probably grew up with little, if any, experience of coping with disorder and confusion, particularly lasting disorder and confusion!

It also means that you may *appear* impatient or demanding when things don't go according to plan. However, what singles tell me is that they're not so much impatient as they are anxious and a bit afraid. They fear the loss of control and predictability they're used to. Singles will often remark that they don't want things 'to get out of control'. My clinical experience suggests that as a result, you singles are also more prone than others to obsessionality – that is, the need to keep everything in order and just so. The singles I've worked with often talk about how uncomfortable, even frightened, they feel when things don't seem clear or when they're unable to predict and understand what's going on around them.

## The older single

Throughout this chapter I refer to singles 'nowadays'. What I mean by this is singles who were born after 1961, the year in which the contraceptive pill was introduced in the UK. This allowed women to choose, really for the first time, how many children they'd like to have, and – to some extent – when to have them.

But what about those singles among you whose birth predated such choices? Is your birth-order profile so different from that of those who were born after 1961?

All singles have some advantages over children born into larger families, regardless of whether their parents chose to have only one child or that was simply what happened. You will all have had relatively more time in adult company, the language you heard would have been richer and more sophisticated and you'll have benefited from comparatively more of the family resources. The latter might mean that you were offered more extra-curricular activities, given more opportunities to travel and, therefore, learned more about the wider world and so on. Because of these enriching privileges, you would have been more likely than other children to do well at school.

All singles probably grew up in a less chaotic household as well, because there were fewer children around. This, in turn, means that you're likely to be more organised, less tolerant of disorder and more of a perfectionist – and again, this applies whether you grew up before or after the introduction of oral contraception. You'll also identify more naturally with people who are older than you, and find it easy to spend time on your own.

So far then, the picture is similar for all singles. However, if you're an older single, you are likely to differ from those born post-1961 in two important ways: firstly, you probably found it relatively more difficult to socialise with your peers, and secondly, you may have felt less self-confident than the younger singles – at least when you were growing up. But why is this?

Parents of older singles were not encouraged to ensure that their child mixed with their peers – at least not as much as they are today – so, older singles had fewer chances to learn social skills. Furthermore, some parents of older singles felt uncomfortable and worried about mixing with other families because they felt they would be considered the 'odd one out'. That meant their child grew up with parents who were more anxious than their modern counterparts, who don't feel so unusual.

However, because all singles tend to be logical, practical and fairly self-sufficient, you 'older' singles could find ways to compensate for any lack of social confidence. You probably developed hobbies and interests to a high degree and, through these activities, you may have met like-minded individuals, some of whom may have become good friends. Therefore, although when you were younger you may have been less confident than the young singles today, age – and the wisdom and experience that come with it – will no doubt mean that those differences have diminished over the years.

## The Single's Guide to Choosing a Partner

You're probably familiar with the saying that opposites attract, and in your case this is almost certain to be advice well heeded. A survey in the US has suggested that when it comes to birth order, the most compatible match is one between a single and a last born. A single will enjoy the unconventional approach of a last born, who will introduce a sense of adventure into the relationship. At the same time, the last born will benefit from the organised and conscientious single who'll take charge and make sure that deadlines are met and that the practicalities of life are sorted out.

A single and a middle born also make a fairly good match. The single will probably want to take charge and make all the major decisions, and the co-operative middle born will be happy to allow his or her partner to devise plans and chart the direction in which to take the relationship.

There's a potential drawback in this match, however. A middle born who's with a single might feel overshadowed and/or over-directed, yet they'd probably not be able to recognise why they're feeling this way. This could lead to feelings of low mood – even depression – in the middle born. In such matches, it would be particularly important for the couple to take some time, on a regular basis, to talk through their plans and ideas with each other, and to make sure that what's happening feels right to both of them.

The most difficult match for a single is probably with another single. Each partner is a relative novice when it comes to knowing how to get on well with equals and to read other people's emotional signals accurately, so the potential for misunderstandings is great. Both will wish to be in charge, and each of them would probably find it difficult to accept directions from the other. Furthermore, if the two partners tended towards perfectionism, then both of them will be vulnerable to driving themselves too hard, because there'd be no one on hand to put on the brakes and to encourage periods of rest and play.

A single and a first born won't get on together easily either, for many of the same reasons that I've just described for two singles. Although the first born would be quite socially aware and would therefore be sensitive to their partner's emotional needs, they're also competitive as you know, so they'd be likely to challenge their single partner for the upper hand in the relationship. This could mean that what might have been a simple lack of clarity turns into an unpleasant competition. If this describes your situation, I suggest you each look for places to excel outside your relationship to take off some of the competitive pressure between you. You might also 'divide' the responsibilities of the household between you, rather than sharing them.

As I've said before, any two people who love one another *can* work together well and enjoy a fulfilling relationship if they respect one another and are prepared to work hard at it. However, if the match is complementary (single plus last born or middle born) rather than competitive (two singles or a single plus first born), it will be easier to achieve harmony.

## The Single's Guide to Choosing a Career

You singles work best on your own, as I'm sure you've already figured out. If, on the other hand, you must work as part of a team, or if indeed you choose to do so, you'll almost certainly be happiest if you can be in charge of your department or your team.

Because you're generally able to motivate yourself, you can set and meet your own deadlines without the help of others to chivvy you along. Also, because your motivation to succeed has little to do with competing against others (only, if anything, against yourself), you're likely to be less stressed than would, say, a first born who's working alone to meet deadlines. You'll also find it relatively easy to do your work without constantly comparing yourself to others. And because you enjoy the praise that comes with achievement, you'll be happiest if anything you do well can be easily recognised as your own, so that you personally receive the credit.

There are only two real drawbacks to choosing to work alone if you're a single. The first is your tendency towards perfectionism. This might cause you to demand of yourself standards that are unrealistically high, and there'd be no one around to point that out to you. You could, therefore, be prone to wearing yourself out needlessly by doing far more than is necessary or good for you.

A second problem could arise if you need to market your products or services directly to the public. Because you're not as practised at understanding and working out the desires and motivations of other people, you might not know how to present what you have to offer in the most convincing way. For this aspect of your work, it would be wise for you either to engage the help of a middle born or a last born, or to take the time and effort to learn more about how best to market your product or service.

---

### *Famous singles*

- Leonardo da Vinci

- Alan Greenspan

- Franklin D. Roosevelt

- Tiger Woods

## CASE STUDY: **Alex**

Anyone who met Alex would, I suspect, be impressed. He was tall and athletic looking and expensively and beautifully dressed. He had excellent manners, although he could at times seem a bit cool and detached. He was eighteen when he was referred to me for depression and possible OCD (obsessive compulsive disorder).

Alex was at the top of his class at school and studying for his A levels. He hoped to read medicine and to become a doctor just like his mother and father. Although he told me that he didn't have any close friends, he recognised that he was respected by his classmates. He added, however, that he longed to be invited more often to parties and nights out. 'Sometimes I think people are scared of me. I wish it wasn't that way,' he said.

Alex's mother, who'd asked to attend his first consultation with her son, insisted that he'd had a perfect childhood. She and her husband had only wanted one child. She'd conceived Alex when she was in her early forties, and the couple were delighted that he was a boy. He'd attended the best independent schools as a day boy, he'd always done very well, and had never doubted that he'd go into a career in medicine. The only problems she could think of were that sometimes he seemed impatient, and that he was very intolerant of disorder.

Alex's depression had 'come on quite suddenly', according to his mother, during the Christmas holidays just after he learned that he'd been rejected for a place at Edinburgh University. Since then (it was now early February), he'd received acceptances from two other prestigious universities, but this seemed to have made no impression on him. Alex had had his heart set on Edinburgh. Since the rejection, his mother said he'd also taken to getting up a great deal during the night and 'just wandering around'.

When his mother left us, Alex began by explaining the problem he felt he had at night. He said he simply couldn't settle down and fall asleep. 'I keep thinking there's some light I left on, or a note I forgot to make to myself, or that I forgot to brush my teeth or something. It seems like there's always something else I need to get up and check.' He said it could take him up to three hours before he'd finally fall asleep, exhausted. It was becoming increasingly difficult for him to get up for school. His mother had, in fact, taken him to the GP because he'd been too tired to go into school three times in one week.

Alex also wanted to talk about another problem. This concerned university. He'd wanted to go to Edinburgh for as long as he could remember – 'because it's the best, isn't it?' – but also, he said, because he already knew some people there. He told me that if he had to describe the biggest problem in his life, that problem was knowing how to make friends. Although he knew that his class-mates respected him, and although he enjoyed spending time on his own, Alex wanted very much to have the social ease that he felt everyone else possessed. He was, therefore, very worried about starting university in a place that was totally new to him, where he wouldn't know anyone at all. He said that more than anything, he dreaded being 'left out'.

When he was younger, particularly at primary school, Alex said his parents had 'tried really hard to make sure I had lots of friends over'. They'd arranged parties and outings, and no expense had been spared. However during his adolescence, he said he'd longed for more freedom to go out with his mates rather than more privileges at home, but that he'd never felt he could tell his parents for fear of hurting their feelings. 'They've always tried so hard to give me everything they think I want,' he told me.

Alex and I decided that the best place to start working

through his difficulties was to deal with the checking, so that he could get a good night's sleep. We created a written checklist for him to go over – once only – and mark in writing when he'd checked what he thought it was reasonable to check. We also agreed a time limit of ten minutes for all the checking. Alex was delighted with this simple, practical approach – 'I'm so glad you don't think I'm some sort of lunatic!' he said. He was conscientious, of course, and stuck to our agreement. Very soon he was sleeping more soundly and was no longer missing school.

We then began to think about other issues he might wish to work on. He identified three of them: how to feel more at ease with his classmates, how to tell his parents what he really wanted without hurting their feelings, and what to do about next year. We decided to start with his parents, and we thought the best approach was to invite them along to the next session. We agreed that I would ask certain questions that would allow Alex to talk about what he'd most like from them, particularly in the way of greater freedom.

As it turned out, the four of us only met twice, because quite quickly Alex realised that his parents weren't hurt or even particularly upset by his requests. Instead, they were merely surprised that he'd not asked them for these privileges before. They clearly adored their son and trusted him entirely. At the same time, they readily admitted that they weren't au fait with 'what teenagers like to do nowadays'.

It also became clear during our discussions that everyone had perhaps gone their separate ways a bit too much at home, and they were out of touch with one another. It was therefore agreed that the family would share a meal together at least twice a week. On those occasions they would make a point of talking about what was happening with each one of them, and in particular ascertain whether Alex was enjoying – and coping well with – the increased freedom he'd been granted.

Alex felt that the time had now come to turn to the question of social ease, particularly in light of the fact that he'd been granted more freedom to stay out with his friends. We started by identifying the friend he felt closest to, a classmate of his called David. David was also planning a career in medicine, but he was looking forward to taking a gap year first to work and travel. David was the youngest in his family, someone Alex described as 'everybody's friend'. Encouraged by the positive response he'd received from his parents when he was direct with them, Alex agreed to ask David to help him find ways to be asked to join in socially more often with his peers.

When Alex returned for our next session, he said he was 'astonished' at how easy it had been to gain more social invitations. David had been surprised and rather amused when he'd listened to Alex's earnest request. He told Alex that everyone assumed that he preferred to be on his own, that he probably regarded their social antics as 'too juvenile' – but that he knew they'd all welcome his company. Alex told me with great delight that things had started to improve dramatically for him socially.

It was now time to consider what he'd like to do next year. Alex said he still wanted to try for Edinburgh – that as far as he was concerned, 'nowhere else measures up'. During our work together, he'd lost his fear about meeting new people which meant he no longer felt worried about how he'd cope socially if he started university somewhere new. That had not, however, meant that he'd changed his mind about Edinburgh. In fact, he was so clear about his desire to be accepted to that particular university that he'd decided to take a gap year and reapply to

Edinburgh the following year. David had already invited Alex to travel with him along with several other friends, and Alex had readily agreed.

He admitted that he still didn't know what he'd do if he was rejected from Edinburgh a second time. However, he felt that now he was much better equipped to cope with disappointment. 'I imagine that what I'd do is to talk it through with my friends if I'm rejected again,' he said.

This sounded like an excellent strategy to me, and we agreed that there was no need to schedule any further sessions.

## What Alex's experience tells us

It was easy to engage Alex in therapy, primarily because of the qualities he possessed as a single – Alex was articulate, and we were able to communicate easily, and the ideas and suggestions I offered appealed to his logical mind (in partic-ular, he was therefore able to tackle his obsessive-compulsive behaviour early on in therapy). Plus, because I'm older – someone closer in age to his parents – he found it easy to relate to me.

Alex's problems – his intolerance of disorder and his uncertainty about how to make friends – are fairly typical of a single. However, by capitalising on his strong points (his pragmatic approach to problem-solving and his determina-tion to overcome his difficulties) he was able to make excellent progress during our time together. It was a pleasure to watch as Alex learned to value his strengths (his good academic skills, especially), rather than use them only as an excuse to drive himself relentlessly to achieve even more. He also learned to think more flexibly and to accept more uncertainty in his life. Tempering his 'black-or-white' thinking meant that he'd become a much happier person.

## CASE STUDY: **Elizabeth**

More than anything else, Elizabeth had always wanted a large family, although for some time she'd thought that might not happen. She'd been the long-awaited only child of professional parents and had been given the best education and opportunities available. Highly successful at school, she'd had a choice of university places. Her parents had hoped she'd live at home while attending university, but Elizabeth – who felt tremendously constrained by her over-protective parents – chose to go as far away from home as possible. She achieved a First, and then went on to do a PhD. She'd gained a position as a lecturer at another prestigious university upon graduation.

It wasn't until she was thirty-six that she met Andrew. They were married two years later, and at last Elizabeth felt she could start her longed-for family. To both of their delight, she fell pregnant within six months. David, a healthy baby boy, was born shortly after her thirty-ninth birthday.

Acutely conscious of her biological clock, Elizabeth began trying for a second child almost as soon as David was born. However, this time she wasn't so lucky – it took nearly two years before she conceived again. This pregnancy seemed different from her first. She was uncomfortable and in pain almost from the start. At thirteen weeks she discovered that she had an ectopic pregnancy. She underwent emergency surgery, and was told that she was highly unlikely to conceive again.

Elizabeth ignored medical advice to give herself plenty of time to recover from major surgery, and threw herself instead into learning all she could about surrogacy and adoption. Four months later she collapsed at work with exhaustion. Her GP signed her off work for three months and urged her to have some therapy to help her face up to and come to terms with what had happened over the last year. At last, she agreed to stop 'running'. At that point we met for her first session of therapy.

By this time, Elizabeth was thin and wan, and extremely depressed. She cried frequently during the session, and referred to herself as a total failure. She viewed herself only in terms of her inability to produce the large family she'd always dreamed of, and refused to acknowledge any other of her many achievements.

We decided to meet weekly and always at the same time because, Elizabeth said, she needed something predictable in her schedule. She'd also agreed to meet with a nutritionist to help her regain her strength. Her GP also suggested a series of regular appointments. At last, Elizabeth stopped focusing on trying to reach 'goals' and began to accept help from others.

As Elizabeth started talking about her childhood, she became aware of how lonely and isolated she'd felt. She'd longed to be with other children, but her doting parents had wanted to be with her as much as possible. She said that at times, she almost felt smothered, yet she felt unable to assert herself because she knew her parents thought they were doing the best for her. But she'd vowed never to allow a child of her own to feel so lonely – hence her desperate desire to have more children.

Although she spoke at length about the children she'd not had, at every opportunity I encouraged Elizabeth to start telling me more about David as well. During these discussions she began to see that, in her desperate attempt to give him what she believed she hadn't been given herself, she was, in fact, failing to show her son how much she loved and cared for him. I asked her if she'd ever considered how things might look from where he stood – that perhaps this little boy might not wish to share his parents with more brothers and sisters. It was quite a breakthrough when she suddenly realised that she'd been looking at the world entirely from her own point of view.

We talked, too, about what a good husband she had in Andrew. He was fifteen years older than she was, the third son of four boys. He was relaxed, sociable and easy-going, and he loved taking David to see friends and relatives who also had young children. He adored his wife, and was for ever praising her for her good sense, energy and organisational skills. Initially, Elizabeth would only comment that she felt envious of Andrew's carefree outlook on life. However, the more she described their relationship, the more she realised that she needn't fear for David. He would never feel as cut off from his peers as she had because he had a very sociable and sensitive father who could see life from a child's point of view.

Gradually, Elizabeth began to realise that if she wanted to feel fulfilled, she was focusing on the wrong thing. There was no need to increase the number of children she and Andrew had. All she had to do was to let herself enjoy her son, and to follow her husband's lead whenever she was unsure as to whether she was being overprotective. She began to trust that together they could raise a happy and sociable child, and that the number of children they might have had little bearing on this. It was this realisation that allowed Elizabeth to stop pushing herself towards her rigid 'goals', and begin to embrace happily the circumstances of her life as it was.

## What Elizabeth's experience tells us

Like many singles, Elizabeth was intelligent and knew how to use that intelligence to win academic success. However, she had not applied her considerable talents to her own life. She'd decided – without considering alternative possibilities – that the only way her son could avoid the loneliness that she'd experienced as a child was to provide him with lots of brothers and sisters. Because she was a single and had grown up in a world of adults, Elizabeth didn't think to look at the world from a child's point of view.

Furthermore, her tendency to be a perfectionist – another characteristic typical of singles – meant that because she felt she had not 'succeeded' in one area of her life (that is, in having the number of children she'd wished for), she'd concluded that she was a 'total failure' in every way.

After her operation, instead of taking the time she needed to recover fully and think through all the options still open to her and Andrew, she'd driven herself relentlessly to adopt children, until her body could take no more and she collapsed with exhaustion. Only then did she start to make use of her ability to think more flexibly about her situation. At that point, it dawned on her that there was more than one possible solution to her dilemma and that, in truth, she already had what was necessary to raise a happy, well-adjusted child.

## Singles in a Nutshell

Singles, once those who were most likely to feel left out and lonely because they were so few, are now a good deal more common and are likely to be happier and more socially skilled than ever before.

To sum up, here is a list of the characteristics most often associated with singles today:

- Good academic abilities and strong communications skills

- High levels of self-confidence

- A preference for the company of older individuals rather than peers

- The ability to spend time alone and to enjoy that time

- Well-developed powers of logic and good organisational skills

- Unease or discomfort when socialising with peers, and a tendency to feel misunderstood by them

- A tendency to perfectionism

- A low tolerance for disorder

We've now looked in detail at the four main birth-order positions and the characteristics that distinguish them. Next, in Part Two, we'll consider the other important factors that have helped to shape you and influenced your birth-order profile.

# PART TWO

# Other Major Influences On Character

Chapter Five

# Your Parents

Until you were at least five or six years old, the most important people in your life were your parents (I'll be using the term 'parents' to denote your main carers, whether or not they were your biological parents). It won't surprise you, therefore, to learn that even as a baby you were acutely aware of their attitudes and feelings – most of all, their attitudes and feelings about you – and that you wanted very much to please them. In particular, between the ages of about three and six (that's the period during which we lay down the foundations of our 'self-concept' – the beliefs we have about ourselves) children copy almost everything their parents do or say. I think there's no doubt that, apart from your own genetic makeup, no other factor comes even close to your parents' effect on shaping your character.

In this chapter I'm going to examine in detail those aspects of parents' own history – as well as their behaviour, feelings and beliefs – that exert the most powerful influences on their offspring.

## Your Parents' Own Birth-Order Positions

As a general rule, we understand best that which we ourselves have experienced. Therefore, parents are likely to feel that they understand most easily the child who's in the same birth-order position they were in. You'll often hear parents say things like, 'Oh I know how Richard feels. I know all about the pressures of being the eldest,' or, 'Well, I know why she's so naughty. I was the youngest, too.' This can be beneficial in some ways, because the child who shares their parent's birth-order position may feel understood, or may be given some extra leeway when they make a mistake.

More often, however, sharing a birth-order position with one or both of your parents is actually not so beneficial. Without even realising it, the parent whose position matches your own may have demanded too much of you, encouraging and sometimes even pushing you to do the things that they regretted not having done, or to do things better than they did. At times, perhaps you may also have felt *too* well understood! That is, you may have felt like you were being second-guessed all the time by a parent who thought he or she knew exactly how you were feeling. You might also have been expected to be more like that parent than you wanted to be.

On balance, I feel that the position that most often offers an individual the greatest freedom to become him or herself is the one that matches that of his parents' favourite sibling when they were children. So for example, if your parent is a first born and got on best with their youngest sibling, it is likely that he or she would have been most indulgent towards the youngest of their own children.

Unfortunately, however, that formula works the other way round as well: if a parent disliked one of their siblings, he or she may have unknowingly transferred those feelings on to whichever of their own children occupied the same birth position. It sounds improbable, I know, but it does happen.

There will almost certainly have been other attitudes that stemmed directly from your parents' own experience of childhood as well. For example, consider a woman who grows up only with sisters and then, when she has children herself, she has a son. She might well conclude that she can't understand boys very well. Therefore, when that son misbehaves, she might say something like, 'Well, that must be what boys do. I wouldn't know.' As a consequence, he'd be treated more leniently than any daughters she might have. Similarly, a father who grew up with only brothers is likely to be more indulgent towards a daughter than any sons he might have.

Often the most demanding and exacting parents are those who were themselves singles. Because they didn't experience another person's childishness (because there were, of course, no siblings in the house) they're likely to have a low tolerance for immaturity and juvenile antics, constantly chiding their children to 'act more grown up'.

## The Relationship Between Your Parents

Your character will also have been affected by the relationship between your parents: how easily they got on with each other, how well they communicated with one another and so on. Here, once again, birth order has a role to play. It's often been said that the partnerships that are most harmonious are the 'complementary' ones – that is, a first born marrying a youngest or middle born (particularly if those relative birth positions were occupied by well-liked siblings in each partner's own family). As a general rule, these combinations make for the most compatible and effective parents. One takes charge, and the other is happy for that to happen.

The most fraught situations are usually those where both parents occupied the same birth-order position in their own families. In particular, two first borns are likely to find it difficult to co-parent because they are both used to being in the position of most responsibility, and each of them wants to take charge. The other potentially volatile match is between two singles, because neither will have been forced to compromise for the sake of an equal.

Last borns often expect others to look after them. Therefore, if two last borns have children together, they may both feel quite helpless when trying to address the problems that all parents face at times. If you grew up with two last borns for your parents, you probably remember things being fairly chaotic at home. No doubt you and your siblings also pushed hard at the limits your parents set for you, simply because you realised that you could probably get away with it.

Finally, middle borns are usually happy to accept compromises and to let others take the lead when it comes to making decisions. Therefore, a middle born and a first born or a single are likely to work well together as parents. If, however, your parents were both middle borns or one was a middle born and the other a last born, you probably have memories of a less-than-orderly household, with parents who had difficulty making decisions. Nevertheless, that household was probably one where the lack of order was well tolerated, and one in which you felt able to explore your own interests and talents.

If you are in one of the potentially difficult partnerships I've just described or if your parents were, please don't despair! It doesn't mean that it's impossible for such partnerships to work, nor are they necessarily damaging to the children. It simply means that there's likely to be more tension and greater difficulties when it comes to finding compromises, so the children in those families grow up in a more highly charged atmosphere than they might otherwise have done. That, in turn, means they're more likely to be tense and anxious themselves. Bear in mind, however, that they only have a higher *chance*. It's by no means a certainty that this will happen.

If you'd like to learn more about the best and the most difficult matches in relation to the various birth-order positions, take a look at the Guide to Choosing a Partner sections in each chapter of Part One.

## *Flashbulb moments*

Besides the various influences on character that we'll examine here in Part Two, there is an additional influence which, albeit not so common, can, none the less, exert an extremely dramatic effect. They're what I call 'flashbulb moments' – events that occur totally unexpectedly, but which change for ever the way you feel and think about certain aspects of your life.

A flashbulb moment may be a world event or it may be something much more personal, such as the death of a parent or sibling (see page 130). A community event might also be a flashbulb moment – one that alters the way in which a neighbourhood or town or social group considers its future (see page 158). In general, such occurrences exert a negative influence, making us more cautious or fearful afterwards. However, flashbulb moments can also occasionally be extremely liberating and positive. For example, when a genetic breakthrough takes place or medical treatment becomes available that brings better health to your family (a personal moment), or when a victim of a natural disaster is discovered still alive (a world event).

If you were to conduct a survey today asking people to recall their most recent flashbulb memory, I'd imagine the most common one would be the collapse of the twin towers in New York on 11 September 2001. From that moment, the notion of terrorism became one of the most frightening of all modern phenomena, its influence extending to new government legislation, the way security is conducted at airports across the globe, how tourists feel about travelling and so on.

Here are some examples of world events that acted as flashbulb moments for me:

I must have been seven or eight years old and was watching the news on TV with my parents in America. I remember very clearly seeing people pushing over school buses full of children. I can still hear the children screaming and the angry adults cursing and shouting. I could not understand why anyone would try to hurt little children.

Only later did it register that those children were black and that what I had seen must have been one of the early attempts to integrate schools in America. However, this realisation only dawned on me through my second flashbulb memory, which was the announcement of Martin Luther King Jr's assassination.

I don't know why those two events made such a tremendous impact on me. I'm white, my family background is middle class and my parents weren't liberal. However, they changed my way of thinking and, therefore, my life, creating in me a relentless desire to try to understand how one group of people can consider another inferior simply because of some physical characteristic. Thus, these flashbulb moments made me a very different person from the one I might have been.

If, as was the case for me, an event seems completely unjust and if it's totally unexpected, and if the nature of what happens means that you identify closely with those affected, then that event – that one moment – can affect the way you regard the world around you as well as what you'll expect in future – for ever. In so doing, it changes your character and exerts a lasting influence on your birth-order characteristics.

## Parenting Style and Beliefs

In the 1960s and '70s there was a surge of interest about the relationship between the way parents raise their children – or what psychologists refer to as parenting 'styles' – and the corresponding levels of self-confidence and happiness of those children. The leading researcher in this field was Diana Baumrind, and her work still stands strong today.

What Baumrind did was to identify three dimensions of parenting:

- a warm vs a hostile attitude towards the children

- a restrictive vs a permissive approach to discipline

- consistent vs inconsistent enforcement of discipline.

She and her colleagues found that parents who were warm towards their children (i.e. genuinely interested in and respectful of their needs and opinions) but who, at the same time, remained in control of discipline and set clear limits, tended to raise children who were co-operative, friendly and confident, whatever their birth-order position. These parents also had high – realistically high, that is – expectations for their children.

My own clinical experience has certainly confirmed these findings. In particular, I've found that those parents who are consistent in the rules they set and uphold produce individuals who find it relatively easy to set limits for themselves and to know when they've done a good job. If their parents were also warm towards them, they, in turn, find it easy to congratulate themselves and to feel proud of their accomplishments. They also find it relatively easy to pick themselves up and try again when they've failed.

When parenting is consistent and warm, all of the children in that family tend to be confident and self-assured, regardless of their birth position. When parenting is consistent but less warm, the children tend to be self-confident, but also rather judgmental of themselves and others.

On the other hand, when parents' behaviour is more chaotic and the rules of discipline shift constantly, their children tend to be highly anxious. Those children are likely to be fearful of feeling 'out of control' themselves and are often pitifully anxious to please others – and this tends to be true even if their parents are warm and loving towards them.

If parents are cold towards their children, then those children almost always suffer from low self-esteem. They also tend to be extremely critical of themselves, feeling as if nothing they do is ever good enough, and they focus far more on their shortcomings than they do on their assets. They also tend to assume that everyone else is more important or better in some way than they are.

Because your parents' (and your own) beliefs about how to parent well would have been quite deeply ingrained and because they felt like general rules, they would have been applied to all the children in the family. That means every one of you, regardless of birth order, was subjected to these rules and ways of enforcing them. Your birth-order characteristics are certainly still there, but they may at times be harder to detect, particularly if the parenting style you grew up with was harsh or inconsistent.

Whether your parents were consistent or inconsistent about disciplining you would have had an incredibly strong effect on your self-esteem. Equally, whether they were warm or cold would also have affected you powerfully – particularly with regard to any tendency to pick out and focus on the best or the worst in yourself. How restrictive or permissive your parents were seems to have less of an effect on character, although it's worth noting that extremely restrictive parents tend to produce individuals who demand high – often unrealistically high – standards for themselves and for others.

## Your Parents' Interests

It's so much easier to get along with others and to find things to do together if you all share similar interests. So it was for your parents – they will have inclined naturally towards those of you who shared their passions and aptitudes. This causes so much guilt among parents (and also sometimes resentment in children) – but only because they confuse compatibility with love; these two often go together, but not always, and they're certainly not the same thing. Your parents no doubt loved all of their children, although they might have found it easier and more satisfying to spend time with some than with others.

As I pointed out earlier, young children look up to and try to emulate their parents, so quite often you and your parents probably did share similar interests, simply because you became involved in what they enjoyed through imitating them. However, if an interest requires a certain skill – say, the ability to play a sport or a musical instrument – and if one of your parents was extremely able in that particular sphere, it may have been harder, if not impossible, to share that interest with them, especially when you were first learning it yourself. This is because that talented parent may have inadvertently made you feel inadequate, at least initially.

Paradoxical though it seems, it takes great sensitivity on the part of a parent to teach their child something if they're already very good at it themselves. Often, the individuals who grow up feeling most isolated from their parents are those whose parents are extremely able. This will be particularly true for those of you who are first borns, because you tend to be the most competitive and at the same time the most sensitive to parental criticism.

## Parenting tip: Encourage effort more than achievement

The best way to encourage your children to explore and develop their own talents is to praise them for their efforts rather than for their achievements. Give them your time – your full and focused attention; listen or observe them whenever you can, and avoid showing them 'the right way' to do whatever it is they're trying to do, particularly if you're skilled in that regard yourself. Instead, help them find a tutor, a coach or whatever will allow them to develop their interests. Parents who work with their children rather than (inadvertently) competing with them produce the most confident children, and also those who are most willing to try new things.

## The Nature–Nurture Issue

Our parents' own personalities are very important when it comes to shaping our character. There are, however, some characteristics that apparently exist from the moment we're born, and it's difficult if not impossible to change them.

If certain of your innate characteristics clashed with some of your parents', it may have caused all of you great anxiety, and, in particular, it probably made your parents feel guilty. Parents often tell me that they find one of their children more difficult than the others and that this makes them feel tremendously anxious. Once again, these parents are confusing compatibility with love.

It would have been perfectly natural if either of your parents had found it more difficult (or easier) to get along with one of their children compared to the others – and, in fact, that needn't in itself have made any difference to their ability to parent well. The anxiety that this awareness generated, however, could have been a problem. If your parents felt anxious whenever they were dealing with their less compatible child, then the chances are high that that child developed into an anxious and less-than-confident adult, someone who's now prone to feelings of guilt and over-responsibility. This is because when young children sense that something's not right – particularly with their carers – they'll automatically assume that it's because of something they've done wrong. If left unchecked (that is, if this happens frequently and they're never reassured), they'll grow up feeling chronically anxious, and will readily assume the blame when things go wrong.

On the other hand, the most confident individuals are those who grow up in homes where they feel loved and supported, whether or not they have much in common with their parents. Usually, the most creative individuals are last borns, as you've already learned. However, if, as a child, you were offered every opportunity to cultivate your own talents and abilities, whether or not your parents shared these with you, it is likely that you will have been able to develop them, regardless of your birth-order position.

## CASE STUDY: **Jackie**

Jackie was thirty-three when she was referred to me for depression and low self-esteem. She'd worked in a number of jobs since leaving school, none of them apparently related to any of the others. Jackie told me that what depressed her most was that she felt she was 'going nowhere'. She'd take on a new job with great enthusiasm, but then within about six months she'd feel disillusioned and disappointed and start looking for something else.

Jackie was the youngest of four children. She described her parents as 'distant and very busy'. They were both professional musicians – her mother played the violin and her father the cello – and they travelled a great deal for their work. Jackie and her brother and sisters had grown up largely in the care of a series of au pairs and child minders.

Although she was encouraged to do A levels, Jackie had left school at sixteen. Since then, she'd worked as a PA, administrative assistant or something similar in her many jobs. She told me, however, that she didn't really enjoy that sort of work; she just did it because she knew she could easily obtain work in that area.

What emerged after several sessions was that Jackie had always wanted to be a musician herself. She, like all her siblings, had been given piano lessons as a child. However, whenever her parents heard her practising they'd come in and 'help' her, playing the pieces perfectly and sighing whenever she seemed to be slow to catch on. When she left home, she'd bought a second-hand piano and taught herself to play jazz and blues, styles her parents didn't much approve of, but ones that she was surprisingly good at. Freed from their criticism and superior ability, she'd found a niche where she truly excelled.

As she gained in confidence during our time together, Jackie gathered the courage to look for work as a session musician. Years later she contacted me with the happy news that she'd moved to New York and was playing as a professional jazz musician.

## Your Parents' Own Upbringing

Another important factor that made a difference to the way your parents raised you is the way they were parented themselves. If you're a parent yourself now, I'm sure you can recall any number of occasions when you've found yourself doing or saying something to your children exactly in the way you remember it happening to you. Again, this is quite natural – we don't generally learn how to parent in any formal way, so we tend to draw on the experiences we have of being parented ourselves. Most of the time, you're probably either parenting just as you yourself were parented, or you may have reacted against certain parental practices that you disliked, and now instead you parent your own children in a totally opposing style. Either way, you may not have stopped to think things through and create what you believe to be your own best approach to raising children.

Furthermore, unless you do stop and think about it, you're likely to hold certain beliefs and values simply because your parents held them and repeated them to you often. You may now realise with a shock that those beliefs or attitudes aren't right for you at all now.

## Parenting tip: Consider your own upbringing

It's important that you take time to think about how you were raised. If you suspect that any particular beliefs or attitudes you hold aren't really your own but are, instead, views you've adopted from your parents without thinking, then it would be wise to reconsider them. If it seems sensible, change your opinion. This is especially important if any of those beliefs or attitudes you hold seem inconsistent with the rest of your belief system.

## Important Events in Your Parents' Lives

Major upheavals in parents' lives will have an impact on their children's character. We'll examine the effect on the other children of the death of a sibling in Chapter Seven, but there are other possibilities as well. For example, if one or both of your parents lost their job, or if they lost one of their own parents or some other loved one, they may have become depressed for a time. Psychologists know that if this happens to the main carer of a very young child, that child may not show much interest in socialising for a time and/or he may not learn to speak as rapidly as his contemporaries.

Fortunately, children are incredibly resilient, so when that parent recovers the child is quite likely to make up for lost time. However, as adults, those children may find that they're more sensitive than others to mood changes in the people they love in particular, and sometimes to everyone else as well. It's important that such individuals remain aware of their heightened sensitivity, and resist any inclination to over-react when those around them are upset.

There are other events in parents' lives that can affect their children's character as well. If one of your parents changed jobs and then spent a great deal of time away from home, this may have created a feeling of distance or even resentment between you. If the absent parent was of the opposite gender to you, it may even have created in you a longing to be loved by an older partner.

Don't, however, jump to conclusions too easily! This is only one of a number of possible reasons why someone might choose a partner who's much older. You've already learned, for example, that singles tend to feel more comfortable in the company of individuals who are older than they are. Therefore, if you're a single and you chose a partner who's several years your senior, it may be because you're drawn through a sense of familiarity and comfort to older people. And, of course, a person can be attracted to someone for reasons that have nothing to do with age or how they were parented!

Nowadays, separation and divorce are two of the most common events that can have a profound effect on your character development. We'll look at this in detail in Chapter Eight.

## Death of a Parent

It's worth mentioning a particular catastrophic event that appears to have an unexpected effect on some children – that is the death of a child's father in particular, although that of either parent is, of course, devastating.

If a mother dies while her children are growing up, in most cases these children lose their primary caregiver. The consequences can be disastrous, and they're always far-reaching. Mercifully, however, it seems that most families and those who support them through their loss are aware of the potential effects of losing your mother, and they make tremendous efforts to try to compensate and support the children as best they can.

If a father dies, however, others may sometimes feel more at a loss about how to respond. It's interesting to note that one result of a father dying before his children reach adolescence is that they are more likely to become highly ambitious and achievement orientated – and this is particularly true of boys. If you acquaint yourself with the lives of highly successful, very driven men, I think you'll find that more of them lost their fathers when they were young than you'd expect by chance alone.

## CASE STUDY: **Fraser**

Fraser referred himself to me because he said he was suffering from burnout. Judging by outward appearances, he had an enviable, highly successful career. He told me, however, that it gave him little, if any satisfaction to think about how many promotions he'd had. He said he enjoyed the moment when he was told of a promotion or a salary rise, but that the satisfaction never lasted. Almost immediately, he'd be thinking about the next advancement. When I asked Fraser what he hoped to achieve by the time he retired he seemed extremely surprised, and said he'd never thought about this!

Fraser was one of three children, and despite his apparent desire for achievement and success, he was not a first born. He had two older sisters, six and eight years older, both of whom were married and worked part time.

Fraser's father had died in an industrial accident when Fraser was ten. His parents had been very close and his mother was devastated. She had not worked during the marriage, but on her husband's death she took employment as a school secretary. Fraser said she'd been an 'incredible' mother, completely devoted to her children. She'd never remarried.

Fraser began to realise that he'd started driving himself to overachieve not long after his father died. He began to see that he'd been trying to please someone who couldn't let him know how proud he felt, which was why Fraser never felt satisfied with any of his many accomplishments.

When he began to give himself credit for his achievements, and to start thinking about the way he wanted to chart his career path, Fraser's interest in work and his self-confidence began to revive.

## Birth-order Characteristics and Your Parents: a Summary

The way you were parented will have had a profound effect on your character. The result is often simply to enhance the characteristics typical of your birth-order position. Sometimes, however, what parents did or what happened to them when you were growing up (for example, with regard to how consistent they were when enforcing the limits they set for you; or if your father died when you were still quite young) will impact strongly on 'typical' birth-order characteristics. The outcome could mislead anyone who's trying to guess your birth-order position.

It's of vital importance, therefore, if you wish to put your typical birth-order characteristics into a meaningful context, that you ask yourself about your parents, what their passions and interests were, how they were parented themselves and what was going on in their lives when you were growing up.

It's time now to take a close look at how your siblings can affect your birth-order characteristics.

# Chapter Six

# Your Siblings

The rate at which a plant grows and whether it will thrive cannot be determined simply by observing the plant in isolation. It's also necessary to consider that plant's companions – that is, what else is growing around it at the same time. For example, will the neighbouring plants overshadow the one we're studying so that it can't get enough sunlight? Will the other plants take away most of the nutrients it needs to reach its maximum height? It's useful to think of siblings in a similar way.

## How Your Siblings Can Influence Your Character: the Crucial Factors

You won't really learn everything you'll need to know about your character unless you take some time to think about the people you interacted with on a daily basis when you were growing up and the relationship you had with each of them. To help you sharpen up your birth-order profile, it's important to take a close look at your siblings.

## The age gaps between you

Prospective parents often ask what age gap is 'best' for their children. My answer is that it's the one that they as parents are happiest with, and that's because every age gap has its own merits and difficulties, and the single factor that allows the merits to outweigh the difficulties is parental attitude to the age gaps between their children. So for example, some parents might moan about a five-year age difference because their children's very differing needs create twice the work for them, whereas other parents might delight in that gap because it allows them to focus fully on the needs of each child, given that those needs will be so different. Similarly, some parents might decide that their unplanned thirteen-month age gap is terrible because both children are so often needy simultaneously – particularly at night – while others would rejoice in that small age gap because the children can share so much of their care.

When it comes to age gaps, parents' opinions about how desirable a particular spacing is will swamp all other factors, so much so that we can safely say that your parents' attitude to the age gap between you and your siblings is what's determined whether you consider it to be a 'good' or a 'bad' one.

That said, I'm sure it would help those who have not yet had children, as well as those who are re-examining their own childhood, to consider how different age gaps are perceived by siblings.

> ### *Parenting tip: Accentuate the positive*
>
> Whatever the age gap between your children, look for and talk up the advantages in that spacing. You might comment, for example, on how wonderful it is that your second born is so much older than his little sister, because he's able to help his sister in so many ways. Or tell your two closely spaced daughters how nice it is that they're at the same school for so long. Make sure you do this even if the spacing was unintentional, or even if it was planned, but has since turned out to be problematical. That way, each of your children will feel special and wanted.

If you are part of a close gap – that is, less than two years – it means you had a playmate and a companion much of the time when you were growing up because your developmental stages and interests no doubt overlapped. If you're the elder, you were less likely to have felt 'dethroned' and jealous when your new brother or sister arrived – at least when you look back now on your childhood – because it will be difficult to remember the exact point at which you lost the exclusive attention of your parents.

However, if you were near in age to one of your siblings, it also means that you had roughly the same needs at the same time, so there was far more competition and rivalry between the two of you. That, in turn, means you're more likely to have argued with and felt jealous of that sibling as you grew up.

A four-and-a-half-year age gap (or more) is generally enough to ensure that the needs of any two siblings won't overlap much, so if that was the case for you you'd have been less often in competition for your parents' care and attention. This larger age gap also increases the chances that the younger child – particularly if their gender is different from that of the older sibling – will have been treated as another first born, with the accompanying high expectations and heightened attention from their parents. If you were, in effect, a 'second first born', the advantage for you is that you reaped the benefits of a first born while being spared the heightened anxiety most first borns must endure. This is because your parents, now more experienced with handling babies and children, were more relaxed and skilled when dealing with you.

The effect of any age gap between these two (that is a two to four-year gap) depends largely on the perspective of the family – that is whether they view it as a large or a small one. In other words, the same gap will engender a very different experience from one family to the next.

In my experience, the strongest and most enduring sibling friendships are between those who are closest in age, even if

– and I'd go out on a limb and say *especially if* – they argued and competed a great deal when they were children. The more often we share powerful emotions, even when those emotions aren't positive, the closer we feel to someone and the better we think we know them. Similarly, the more conflicts we work through with someone, the closer we feel towards them. Therefore, if you had siblings who were close in age to you, then you and those siblings are most likely to benefit as adults from close and lasting friendships.

Siblings with a large age gap between them can also feel close to one another later in life, although the quality of that relationship is different from those who are nearer in age. When there's a big gap the relationship is more of a carer/cared-for – or some might even say a parent/child – relationship. The younger sibling feels safe and looked after by the older one, while the older one feels strong and needed.

A close age gap encourages both siblings to develop some middle-born characteristics because the two must learn to find ways to share parental attention and material goods. A larger gap, particularly where one of you is male and the other is female, may mean that both of you will have acquired first-born characteristics. In particular, the younger sibling acquires the positive qualities associated with being first born, but is unlikely to be as anxious or as jealous as her older sibling, as we've seen.

## The gender of your siblings

Even when they try not to, parents will treat their sons differently from their daughters, and they'll also hold different preconceptions about them. Parents are also – quite naturally – excited when the first child of the other gender is born, so that child will in many ways be treated as another first born. Furthermore, when there are more than two children in the family and one is a different gender, that one is likely to receive special treatment and be given more attention than their siblings, who may sometimes be referred to collectively as 'the others'.

It's not hard to see, therefore, that the gender mix of the sibling group makes a difference to the way each individual in the family is treated and how if there's only one sibling whose gender is different, he or she is likely to receive extra parental attention. However, this may be for good or ill! For example, if you were the only boy in your family and you were also a last born, you may have grown up pampered and cosseted by all the women around you, and now be someone who expects women to wait on you. If, on the other hand, you were the only boy and you were the first born, you may have grown up feeling excessively pressured to be a high achiever, particularly if your parents believed that boys are more likely to pursue careers than are girls.

Another way that gender can make a big impact is that pairs of siblings are more likely to compete if they're both the same gender, particularly if they're also close in age. If you're male and you grew up with a sister, you're less likely to have competed with her than if you'd had a brother as your only sibling.

Some combinations can 'minimise' the age gap between siblings and encourage competition and rivalry – in particular, male–female pairings. The reason for this is that girls tend to mature faster than boys, particularly linguistically. Therefore, if you're a male with a younger sister, you may have found that all too early she began to show greater competence and maturity (at least linguistically if not also socially) than you did. This would have led, no doubt, to a heightened competitiveness in your sister, while you may have suffered from a sense of inferiority and lower self-esteem.

Finally, when there are both boys and girls in a family, it seems that the gender-specific characteristics of one group exert their influence on the other. In particular, when there are more males than females in a family, the females tend towards more tomboyish behaviour. When there are more females than males, those males are often more nurturing and emotionally sensitive than other men.

## The number of children in the family

The more children there were in your family, the more socially skilled you'll all be, and the better you'll be at getting your way, if you need to, when you're with other people. This is simply a common-sense observation. On the flip side, however, the more children there were in your family, the less time your parents had to spend with each of you, and therefore the less likely it is that any of you had all your needs met promptly. The effect of this is that those of you who grew up in larger families (with four or more children) – and in particular, the middle borns – will be less likely than others to ask that your own needs and desires are addressed. It's not that you'll necessarily feel hopeless or despondent about this. It's simply that, whenever your requests aren't readily acknowledged, you tend to give up (or at least compromise) more easily than do individuals from smaller families whose requests were more likely to have been heard and heeded straight away.

Those of you who grew up in larger families are likely to prefer the company of peers, as you might expect. This doesn't have quite so much impact on the middle and last borns who, like middle and last borns in smaller families, tend to prefer socialising with peers anyway. But it does soften the tendency of first borns to prefer older companions. So first borns in larger families may as easily become friends with peers as with those who are older than they are; first borns in smaller families, on the other hand, will more often choose friends who are older than they are. When they mix with peers, they'll tend to lead rather than follow.

Another feature of large families is that, as suggested in

the section on gender, the more children there are of the same gender in that family, the more they'll behave in ways that are stereotypical of their gender. So for example, if you grew up in a family of five and all of you are girls, the odds are that you'll behave, think and feel in a more typically 'feminine' manner than if you'd grown up with, say, two brothers and two sisters.

## Multiple births – twins, triplets, etc.

Much of what's been written about birth-order effects on twins is rather confusing. On the one hand, there's an assumption that one twin will take on the role of a first born while the other behaves like a last born. However, this 'finding' appears to be based largely on anecdotes, and it's easy to find numerous exceptions and 'role reversals'.

In my opinion, the most important fact about twins – or any multiples – is that they grow up trying to distinguish themselves from *each other*. That's simply all you need to know, and if you think about this in terms of Darwin's Principle of Divergence (see page 36), it's easy to understand why.

Two individuals who are born at roughly the same time will have many of the same needs simultaneously. If, on top of that, they also look alike, then each will have to work really hard – much harder than they would if they were competing with any other sibling – to distinguish themselves from the other and to make their parents aware of *their* particular needs. If it's just 'the twins' Mum and Dad respond to, then each one of them will probably get the same treatment but with only half the attention. That may not be all that's needed, and it certainly won't be all that's desired.

Therefore, most twins grow up with a strong desire to distinguish themselves from their brother/sister in every way they can. In comparison to the 'twin influence', their birth-order position is far less important.

I think you can see from this discussion why it's so unwise for parents to treat twins as if they're indistinguishable. Each of us is unique, even if our genetic makeup is identical to that of someone else, and even when two people have exactly the same experience at exactly the same time they will be affected by and react to it in different ways.

Nevertheless, although the most powerful effect of being one of twins is that it creates in each twin a desire to be different from the other, twins are also likely to share an extremely close bond. This is true not only because they spend so much time together, but also because they must compete so intensely with one another for parental attention. As it is with any pair of siblings, the more intense the relationship when they're young – whether that relationship was largely positive or negative – the closer their bond is likely to be when they become adults.

## *Parenting tip: See your children as individuals*

If you're raising twins or triplets or any other group of children who are the same age, always try to draw attention to and praise their unique qualities – those that set them apart from their siblings. Avoid referring to them collectively as 'the twins' or 'the triplets' and try to help each one dress and generally appear different from the others, in ways that bring out the best characteristics of each one of them. Children's need to distinguish themselves from their siblings is incredibly powerful, particularly when they're young, and it gives them a better chance to thrive. Therefore, even though it's tempting to dwell on the similarities between twins, it's more important to emphasise their unique strengths, just as it is for any other child.

Twins (or triplets or quadruplets even more so) will exert a powerful effect on their other siblings if there are any, particularly the one who's immediately above or below them in age. Although multiple births are somewhat more common nowadays, probably because many women have children later and perhaps, therefore, need hormonal treatment to boost their fertility, they are still rare enough to be interesting. That means that these children are likely to attract more attention than their siblings, and as a result their siblings are likely to feel left out – neither special nor important. As a consequence, they're prone to feelings of low self-esteem or, on the other hand, to feel driven to over-achieve in an attempt to attract the attention and praise they feel they deserved but didn't get. They may find it difficult to control jealous feelings throughout their lives, particularly when others around them are singled out and praised.

## CASE STUDY: **Richard**

Richard was seven when his mother Sarah came to see me. According to her, he'd been a 'model child' until he was six. He was regarded as the brightest child in his class, and he was popular with everyone. Over the previous six months, however, his behaviour had deteriorated both at school and at home. He was prone to angry outbursts or floods of tears, often quite unexpectedly. There'd also been reports that he was bullying children during play time, particularly girls.

Eight months ago Sarah had given birth to twin girls. She'd thought beforehand about the fact that Richard might feel left out, and had hired an au pair to help out, especially with Richard to give him lots of extra attention. She'd also assumed that, because the twins were girls, Richard would still stand out because he was the only boy.

During our discussions, Sarah realised that although

she'd done well to hire extra help when she knew her hands would be so full, she'd not used that help as wisely as she might. She began to see that what Richard was missing most wasn't so much attention generally as parental attention in particular. She also realised that although he was actually angry with his new sisters, he was also afraid to upset his parents who clearly adored them. He was, therefore, redirecting his anger away from the twins and towards his female classmates.

Sarah's solution was simple. She encouraged her au pair to assume some of the care for the girls so that she and her husband could spend some time with Richard each day. As a result, he stopped bullying other children, resumed his good behaviour at school and was generally a much happier child.

## Siblings who need extra attention

When one member in the family has a disability it means, of course, that that individual will need extra care and attention. Some birth-order theorists have claimed that because of this, the disabled child becomes for all intents and purposes a 'functional last born'.

In my experience, this is utterly unsubstantiated. The character of a child with special needs is shaped far more powerfully by their own innate characteristics, the symptoms of their particular disability, the way they're cared for, and the attitudes of their carers towards the disability. These factors are far more important than the birth-order position they occupy. For example, individuals who suffer from autism and Asperger's syndrome aren't gregarious, nor do they wish to be the centre of attention; most, in fact, prefer as little social interaction as possible. This will be so even if they're a last born, despite the fact that last borns typically seek the limelight socially.

To give you another example, many individuals with physical disabilities know they'll have to struggle that much harder than others to live 'normal' lives. So if they're encouraged by loving carers to believe they have a right to the same privileges as anyone else, and if they're surrounded by able siblings who are good role models, they'll most likely be supremely determined and self-confident, much like a single. I don't believe, therefore, that birth order alone can tell us much about those who have special needs.

However, when one child in the family has a chronic disability, their presence is bound to have a powerful effect on their siblings. The brothers and sisters of someone with special needs are quite likely to be good at nurturing and caring for others and to take on positions of responsibility – in effect, they'll appear to be more like first borns. At the same time, they can also appear rather like middle borns in that they're apt to champion the causes of the less fortunate. They're also more likely than most to be aware of the needs of others and to step aside so that those needs are given priority.

## CASE STUDY: **Anna**

Anna's case is a good example of how birth-order qualities can sometimes be overridden and changed by experience.

Anna was referred to see me because of 'chronic stress, fatigue and depression'. She was a solicitor in a small firm where she worked very long hours and was highly regarded by her colleagues. Anna was well known for taking on 'hopeless' cases, and she had a very good success rate helping such individuals obtain the help or compensation they sought.

I would not, however, have learned about her successes and the respect others had for her unless I'd asked persistently. What Anna told me was that she viewed herself as a 'real disappointment' because she'd failed to get a job working with the most prestigious law firm in her area. She also volunteered to tell me that she didn't get into her first choice of university, the one her parents had both attended.

When I asked her what she liked best about her work, Anna became animated and showed real enthusiasm for the first time. She said that without a doubt, she most enjoyed helping people whom others regarded as 'no hopers'. She said the most satisfying thing in her life was to see someone show real optimism after she'd help them win a case.

Judging from this interview alone, I guessed that Anna was either a first born (because of her high ambitions and references to succeeding in ways her parents probably valued) or a middle born (because of her desire to champion the underprivileged). In fact, it turned out that she's the fourth child, the youngest in her family and the only female. Her older brother was also a solicitor and had moved to New Zealand, so she rarely saw him. Between her and her brother, however, were twin boys, both of whom suffered from cerebral palsy. Much of Anna's childhood had been spent helping her parents care for her brothers. Clearly the combination of having twins and siblings with special needs meant that Anna had begun to believe that she was only 'worthy' when she was wearing herself out on behalf of others and not attending to her own needs. This was in part because this was the role she was most used to taking on, and in part because she was seeking the attention and praise from others that she'd not had in sufficient amounts from her parents.

## The death of a sibling

Understandably, the death of a sibling can have a profound effect on a family. After the initial overwhelming grief and misery that follow the death of a loved one, it is natural to begin thinking of happier times spent with that person and to dwell on their best qualities, while perhaps overlooking their faults. When a parent does this after the loss of a child, the impact of this selectivity of memory on everyone else in the family can be profound. If you had a brother or sister who died when you were young, you may have felt that you had little hope of emulating someone who, in your parents' eyes, became more and more perfect with the passage of time.

For the siblings of a child who has died, trying to be as good as someone who's been idealised and is no longer around to make mistakes can be totally demoralising. It may help to fuel a driving ambition to be successful – with the sole aim of gaining the parental attention and approval that are so badly missed, of course – but it doesn't encourage feelings of contentment or self-confidence.

### *How flashbulb moments can affect character*

As we saw on page 105, flashbulb moments come in different guises. Here's an example of a more personal one, which involves the death of a sibling.

It was an ordinary weekday morning. Gina was getting herself ready for work when the telephone rang. It was her mother. She sounded hysterical, and Gina could barely understand what she was saying. There was something about aeroplanes hitting buildings in New York.

➔

. . . New York. That's when, for Gina, that moment became a flashbulb moment. One of her three older sisters, the one who was closest in age to her, had moved to New York a year earlier to work in advertising. Her bold decision had inspired Gina, and she was hoping to find a job in New York so that she could join her sister.

Gina can recall the five minutes that followed in every detail. She remembers turning on the TV and discovering exactly what had happened, then realising with a cold horror that her sister was almost certainly dead.

From that day onwards, Gina's character changed. Formerly an adventurous, gregarious, rather impulsive young woman, Gina became more anxious and fearful and much less likely to try anything new or unconventional. In short, she became less like a typical last born.

When a child dies, another problem for their siblings is that they may grow up feeling responsible for the death. Children younger than about five believe themselves to be more powerful than they actually are, and they have difficulty imagining that things can happen independently of their own wishes and deeds. It's natural for siblings to be jealous of one another, and it would be extremely likely that the siblings of a sick child would be particularly jealous because that child no doubt received so much extra parental attention, probably at their expense. If that child then died, their siblings may feel that they caused the death by wishing the child was out of the way. It doesn't make sense to us, I know, but young children will readily believe they've caused something to happen simply by wishing it so.

After a time, it may seem that the family recovers from the death of a child. However, siblings' guilty feelings may well endure, buried deep in their unconscious mind. When they grow up they may become overly protective of loved ones, and whenever things go wrong they may automatically assume responsibility and feel overwhelmed with guilt. This pattern can be overcome, but it takes sensitive professional help to bring the memories and the faulty childhood beliefs into consciousness and help sufferers to challenge them.

## CASE STUDY: Vic

After he suffered a heart attack at forty-six, Vic was referred by his GP for some mindfulness therapy (this involves learning how to relax, perhaps to meditate, and to experience present moments as fully and non-judgementally as possible). He was the CEO of a rapidly expanding company, he worked long hours (a fourteen-hour day was not unusual for him) and he rarely, if ever, took as much holiday as he was entitled to take. He was married with two teenage children. He and his wife had separated twice because she said she never saw enough of him.

Vic's enormous, unquenchable drive was not because he was a first born with an exaggerated desire to succeed. He was, in fact, the younger of two boys and his drive to over-achieve became more understandable when he talked to me about his childhood.

He described his parents as 'traditional, strict and a bit old fashioned'. Vic's one brother, James, was four years older than him. He told me his brother was 'much cleverer, more athletic – well, just *better* – than me'. He said that he always knew his parents had favoured James. When James was sixteen, he was killed in a car accident. Vic said his parents never recovered from this loss. He added that nothing he achieved, probably before James died and certainly afterwards, seemed to matter at all to his parents. At the core of Vic's striving was his desire, never fulfilled, to gain his parents' notice and approval.

## Birth-order Characteristics and Your Siblings: a Summary

This chapter has, I hope, helped you to refine and sharpen up the birth-order characteristics associated with your position in the family. By thinking in greater detail about your siblings, as well as the relationships you had with them, you're now in a position to understand more clearly why the 'typical' birth-order characteristics may not match you exactly, and perhaps even why you have one or two characteristics normally associated with birth-order positions other than your own.

In the next chapter we'll take a look at the effects that separation, divorce and remarriage can have on a family, and the impact that those experiences may have had on your birth-order characteristics.

# Chapter Seven

# Shake-ups in the Family

In Chapter Five we looked at the powerful role that your parents can play in the development of your character. In truth, their influence is so central that the way they raised you will have been more important overall in shaping your character than will any other factor. We need, therefore, to spend some time thinking about any big changes in your parents' lives that may have altered the way in which they raised you.

To some extent, we touched upon this subject in Chapter Five when we considered the effect of parental depression and bereavement on their ability to raise children. In this chapter, however, we'll be turning our attention away from changes within parents (their mood state and their outlook on life) to focus on outer changes: moving house, separation and divorce, the introduction of a new partner and possibly the presence of step-siblings are some of the issues we'll be considering in relation to birth order. We'll also look at other changes that can reconfigure the family – in particular, the return of a grown-up sibling and the introduction of an infirm or elderly relative into the household – and the impact that such adjustments have on children in different birth-order positions.

## Moving House

No one finds change easy, particularly a big one, and moving house is considered to be one of the biggest stresses we can ever face. That said, the effect that a move will have on someone's character has more to do with the reasons why the move takes place than with the move itself.

If, for example, your family was obliged to move because one or both of your parents lost their jobs, then the negativity around that event will no doubt have distressed everyone. As a result, you and your family may well have had problems adjusting to their new surroundings, especially if you felt that you were 'forced' to move to the new location. In particular, your eldest sibling may have become more anxious and felt overly responsible for the reactions of the younger children in the family. This would have been even more probable if either or both of your parents became depressed as a result of their job loss. The overall effect would have been for everyone's self-confidence to have taken a knock, and for any family member who was previously optimistic or relatively carefree to have become less so as a result of what felt like an enforced and unwanted upheaval.

On the other hand, perhaps the move was made for positive reasons – your family may have inherited some money, or one of your parents landed a job in a city you'd all always longed to live in. Under those conditions, the knock-on effects would have been more positive. Some of you may have seen this as a chance to make new friends or to reinvent yourself in some way – and I'll bet you've already guessed by now that this is most likely to have been true for the last born among you. The last born is the one who'd have been most likely to consider a big change to be an exciting adventure.

A move that was instigated for positive reasons would also have strengthened the bonds between all of you. This is because we feel closer to people with whom we've shared an adventure, or those who've been with us during a positive change in our lives.

Your age at the time of the move is another important factor. As a rule of thumb, the older you were, the less positive you'll have considered the move to be. Older children – particularly teenagers – find it difficult to leave old friends, and even more difficult to struggle to 'fit in' with a new group who are, no doubt, already well established. At the same time, the move would have been rather less daunting to the last born in your family. Because the youngest has always had to share and compromise with several others, they are more practised at fitting into new social groups.

The number of individuals in your family will also have made a difference to the way in which you reacted to any moves you had to make. The larger your family (and particularly if your siblings are all relatively close in age), the less daunting any adjustments would have seemed. This is because each of you already belonged to a cohesive 'group' (your own family), and of course that group doesn't change when you move, even though friends and neighbours do. It's interesting to note that at the other extreme – that is, if you're a single – the effect of any move would have been less powerful as well. That's because singles and their parents tend to be a fairly self-contained unit, so the effects outside the family unit feel less important.

The number of moves your family made when you were growing up would also have had an impact on your character. As a general rule, the more often a child moves, the less importance he'll attach to long-standing peer friendships – that, of course, only makes sense as an adaptive strategy. If, in addition, you weren't particularly outgoing or self-confident, then numerous moves would only have intensified your sense of isolation. If, on the other hand, you were generally self-confident, then those moves almost certainly enhanced and strengthened your sense of self-reliance and independence.

Finally, it's important to note that the effects of any move on your character will have been most powerfully determined by your parents' attitude. If they prepared you well in advance for any changes, if they emphasised the positive aspects of the move (no matter how few they might have been) and if they remained sensitive to your needs once you'd moved and helped you for as long as it took to adjust to the new circumstances, then you and all of your siblings – regardless of birth-order position – are likely to have benefited from moving. In particular, you'll now be more socially skilled and better able to adjust to change, more so than if you'd never been challenged by a move.

## *Parenting tip: If the family relocates*

If you move house, play up any possible benefits of that move. Point out specific advantages and choose what you enthuse about by trying first to imagine the new neighbourhood through your children's eyes. If your children see that you're in a positive frame of mind about what's happening, they're more likely to adapt well to the new circumstances.

## Parental Separation and Divorce

All children are distressed if their parents separate or divorce, and during nearly thirty years of clinical practice I've not encountered one child who wanted their parents to break up. It's true to say that many have longed for the arguing to stop, and that some have claimed to be much happier once the separation was finalised and things had settled back down. None the less, no child wants their parents to split up.

This is not to say that if someone's in a miserable partnership, one where they've tried to do everything in their power to improve the situation but have failed to see any positive change, that they should soldier on in those miserable conditions 'for the sake of the children'. Children sense prolonged unhappiness and despair in their parents even when parents try to hide those feelings, and this in itself can be damaging to them.

Even so, it's important to recognise how distressing parental break-up is for children. If separation or divorce seem an inevitable step for you, then the most important thing you can do is to acknowledge that although your own relationship with each other is best ended, your shared role as parents must continue. At least then your children will grow up knowing that even in the most distressing circumstances, they were still loved and loveable. I'm sure that if you endured a separation or divorce when you were a child, you know that the *way* in which things were handled was what mattered most – more even than what actually happened.

If your own parents divorced, but afterwards managed to continue to work together in their role as parents, you have much to thank them for. If on the other hand one or both held on to their bitterness long after the break-up and refused to co-operate so that they could parent you well, then you'll tend to overreact whenever you witness or are involved in arguments.

It's imperative to remember that a child is a reflection of both their father and their mother. Therefore, if one parent denies that child access to the other parent or continually derides and criticises their ex, the child will feel that they, too, are being criticised. Shame and guilt – and, often later on, anger for being caught up in a dispute that's not of their making – are the inevitable consequences of this sort of behaviour.

## Parenting tip: The importance of access

Efforts should always be made to allow children access to both parents – although of course, should it be considered dangerous for a child to spend time with one parent, the other parent should make sure this can be done safely, for example by making use of family contact centres.

### CASE STUDY: **Penny**

Penny was referred by her GP for depression. She was thirty-one and had just broken up with her fourth long-term boyfriend. She felt she had no energy and was constantly tearful. Her GP had signed her off work for a month.

Penny told me that her biggest problem was that she didn't know how to find a 'really good man'. She was a pretty woman and obviously socially skilled, so she had no trouble attracting men. However, she said that everyone she met 'eventually lets me down'. She no longer trusted her own judgement, and was beginning to wonder if there would ever be anyone she could truly love.

Penny's parents divorced when she was nine. What she remembered was that her father and mother were constantly rowing, and that eventually her father had fallen in love with another woman. Her mother never met anyone else, never tried to do so, and had never forgiven her ex-husband. She moved away from where he was living so that contact for him with their children would be difficult, and she constantly made excuses as to why Penny and her two younger sisters couldn't see him on contact weekends. She also criticised her ex relentlessly in front of the children, telling them in great detail why and how he'd been such a 'bad husband and useless dad'.

Penny had loved her father. He'd always been kind to her and spent time with her, and she'd missed him terribly. However, after a time she began to wonder if her memories were accurate. Perhaps, she began to think, she was only imagining how she'd wanted her father to be rather than how he really was. Eventually, they'd lost touch.

In our work together, Penny began to see that she'd transferred her longing for and confusion about her father to her current relationships. No one could, of course, live up to the lofty image she'd created in her mind of an ideal partner. And because her mother's constant tirades were so at odds with her own memories, she'd begun to doubt her own ability to judge another person's character as well.

With time, Penny learned how to recognise and accept both the good and the less desirable qualities in the people she'd meet and, on this more realistic basis, to decide whether she wished to get to know them better. She also re-established contact with her father to the delight of them both. As she got to know him, she was able to reconsider her childhood memories and to realise that she could trust her own recollections and judgement after all.

## The principal effects of separation

How, then, does parental separation/divorce affect a child's character? Which children will be most affected? And in what circumstances might the least damage be done?

All children whose parents split up will doubt that there can be such a thing as 'happily ever after'. This will be so regardless of their birth-order position. When they begin to have relationships themselves they're likely to feel less certain than they would otherwise have done with regard to their own feelings as well as those of the person they're attracted to. In effect, they become more cynical. Some, particularly those who felt unloved or unimportant for long periods of time when their parents were warring, or who were denied access to the parent of the opposite gender, may idealise people they're attracted to and rush too quickly into relationships, only then to feel bitterly disillusioned.

My clinical experience suggests that first borns tend to be most negatively affected by parental break-up because they are the ones who are liable to feel the need to look after other family members and to 'put things right' when they are not going well. If the separation is handled carefully – that is, with minimal hostility and bitterness – and parents continue to co-parent responsibly, all of their children, particularly their first born, will be less anxious as a result.

However, if the arguing goes on for a very long time and the separation is laced with blame and harsh criticism, not only will all of the children in that family feel anxious (and perhaps angry as well later on), but the first born in particular may become vulnerable to bouts of depression when they're older. When any of us finds ourselves in situations that are out of our control, where everything we try to do makes little or no difference, and where the distressing circumstances continue for some time or happen repeatedly, we start to feel hopeless about the future generally and to believe that there's no point putting in effort when things go wrong. This is known as 'learned helplessness', and it's a mindset that makes an individual vulnerable to depression. The child that most resembles or feels nearest to the parent who's being most heavily criticised and ostracised from the rest of the family is particularly prone to feelings of helplessness and low self-esteem when parents separate.

Another factor that comes into play is the age of a child at the time of their parents' separation – especially at the time when the arguing and indecision are most acute. As we've seen, children of younger than about five years of age believe themselves to be at the centre of everything that's going on, so they'll react to parental conflict and discord by wondering what they've done wrong. If younger children aren't repeatedly reassured that they're not to blame for a separation, they may develop a habit of blaming themselves whenever things go wrong.

Having said that, the younger the child is when parental separation occurs, the more likely he or she is to accept and adjust to their new situation. When children grow up, however, and particularly once they're teenagers, their peer group becomes a central anchor for them. Therefore, anything that threatens the way they're perceived by their friends or that jeopardises the time they can spend with them causes anxiety and resentment.

## CASE STUDY: The Morgan family

Geoff and Janet Morgan came to see me because they'd decided to separate. There was no one else in the picture for either of them. They'd seen three different couple counsellors during the previous two years and after the third lot of counselling they both felt that things still hadn't really improved. They therefore regarded separation as inevitable. However, they'd come to see me because they wanted to handle the separation in the best way possible for their three children, Megan, fifteen, Josh, six and Peter, four.

Janet had always been at home with the children, so the couple had assumed that all three of them would live with their mum. She planned to move to the town in which she'd grown up so that she could be nearer to her parents.

In our discussions, however, the couple realised that with such an age gap between Megan and her brothers, it wasn't really appropriate to treat all the children in the same way. Megan had a strong group of friends and she loved her school, whereas the boys had only just begun their schooling. At the same time, they knew that because she was a first born and, therefore, particularly eager to please her parents, Megan would agree to do whatever they asked of her.

After further thought and discussions, they decided they'd offer Megan the choice of staying with her father and therefore not having to change schools, or moving with her mother and brothers. Janet knew Megan would still wish to feel close to her mother, so she offered to visit her daughter on alternate weekends so the two of them could spend time together, without Megan having to give up too much of her social life. This compromise allowed Megan to do what she preferred – to stay with her father and be near her friends, but also to see her mother regularly.

## Other effects of parental separation

The changes that result from a separation or divorce can also affect a child's character in other ways. In almost every case, everyone is less well off financially than they were before. Both parents may be forced to move to smaller homes, or if one parent remains in the family home with the children there will be less income to run it. Because the parent(s) need to work harder to make ends meet, their children usually become more aware of the straitened financial circumstances and, therefore, less carefree themselves.

Of course, it's not possible to clone individuals and discover how they'd turn out had their parents not split up. However, I think it's safe to say that, on the whole, children who experience parental separation will be less easy-going when they grow up than if they had not. At the same time, though, they'll be able to adjust to changes more readily. I'd also guess that if children are exposed to prolonged parental conflict, they'll grow up to be less optimistic and more prone to bouts of depression. Once again, although these factors affect everyone in the family, first borns are likely to be worst affected because of their heightened sense of responsibility for others.

Another consequence of parental separation is that the children involved will almost certainly see one parent less often thereafter, and that means that in effect, they have lost one of the two most important role models in their lives. As a result, they may develop an idealised and/or unrealistic concept of how men or women should be. If the absent parent shares their gender, a child may also acquire a less realistic gender identity or, at best, may question and worry disproportionately about their identity. If the absent parent is of the opposite gender to the child, that child may have difficulty forming love relationships because they expect too much of, or 'idealise', their partner. It helps if there are other responsible and happy adults around to serve as positive role models. However, children will always compare themselves to and identify most strongly with their parents. This consequence of divorce – the potential loss of an important role model – affects the sons and daughters in the family differentially, depending on which parent moves out and how often the children see that parent.

The way in which a child's 'base' is established after parental separation is another factor that can make an impact on their character. When children are very young, the carer they're with and the quality of the care they receive are more important than the place where they sleep. However, as children grow up and start to build their own social lives, they want increasingly to base themselves in one safe place. So although almost every child I've worked with tells me that they want to be able to see both parents, none has welcomed the idea of having two equally important homes. For some reason (and I have to admit that I'm not sure what that reason is) older children prefer to live in one home; however, they also want access to both parents. In my experience, a child who's been asked to divide his time equally between two homes – that is, if the division is decided by their parents rather than by themselves – is likely to suffer from feelings of isolation from their peers and to doubt their acceptability in social terms.

It's possible to argue that the effects I've described here – that is, those that arise from prolonged parental conflict and/or separation and divorce – are likely to be temporary, and that they shouldn't, therefore, be thought of as affecting a child's character for the rest of their life. And this may well be true in some cases. However, for the majority of individuals, these effects will change the way they think about life and, in particular, the way they react to stresses in their own adult relationships. That's why if a separation seems inevitable, it's so important that parents handle it with a view to minimising the distress it will cause their children. Furthermore, when they're deciding how to sort out contact, parents should consider each child's needs individually. They have to think about each child's age, gender and birth-order position, because each of these factors will affect the way that the child perceives and reacts to their situation.

## Step-families

Surprising though it may seem, the introduction of a step-parent causes most children less long-term distress than that of step-siblings (as long as that introduction is handled sensitively, of course). Difficulties are minimised when a step-father doesn't try to replace a father, and a step-mother doesn't try to replace a mother, even if these have died. If you had a step-parent and they didn't try to 'fill a gap', but instead allowed you to accept them in your own way, you probably have had a good relationship with them.

Furthermore, if your parent and new step-parent formed a united front and backed each other up with regard to discipline and household rules in general, and if your parent was happier because their new partner moved in, then things probably settled down well. You may even have had a richer life – after all, you now had another person in your life to serve as a positive role model and to love you.

First borns tend to be most affected by the introduction of a step-parent. More often than not, a first born will have assumed a powerful sense of responsibility for the parent they're living with. In some cases, that child even becomes a soul mate for their parent. Therefore, when their parent finds a new partner, the first born may once again feel a tremendous loss, similar to when the second child was born into the family. Making way for someone else once again can stir up all the old jealous feelings.

## CASE STUDY: **Rowan**

Rowan's parents divorced when he was ten. The elder of two, Rowan helped his mother – when she had to increase her hours of work – by doing household tasks and looking after his sister.

He was fourteen when his mother met Stephen. Outwardly, Rowan appeared to be unaffected by this turn of events, and he and Stephen seemed to get on well. However, his mother noticed that he was spending more time alone in his room. When Stephen moved in with the family a year later, Rowan's behaviour began to deteriorate rapidly. He started to miss school and, not long after, his mother noticed ugly scratches on his arms. She made an appointment to see the GP with Rowan, who then referred them both to me.

Fortunately, Rowan's father was still in touch with his son, although face-to-face contact was quite rare. None the less, he, as well as Stephen and Mum, were willing to help in any way possible to make life easier for Rowan.

Our work together was conducted on a number of fronts. First, I told Rowan about an excellent peer counselling scheme that was running at the local family contact centre. Rowan agreed to talk with a teenager there who'd had an experience similar to his own. Also, his mum and Stephen arranged to spend time with Rowan, each of them on their own on a weekly basis. Furthermore, Rowan's dad re-established regular contact with his son. As a result, Rowan's work at school improved and he stopped cutting himself.

## Introducing step-siblings

The introduction of a step-parent is a difficult challenge in and of itself. If, in addition, step-siblings are brought into the equation, the situation will be even more fraught.

If you think about what happens from a 'resources' point of view when two families come together you can understand why. Darwin's Principle of Divergence (see page 36) can help here. The principle states that individuals will compete for the best share of the available resources in their environment. When more people (in this instance, step-children) are introduced into the family, there are suddenly more individuals in that same environment. However, there is not that much more – if anything at all – in the way of additional resources. That means that rivalry and competition can only intensify. So an increase in arguments and disagreements, particularly between siblings and their step-siblings, is almost inevitable.

And what about birth-order characteristics? Are they affected by changes in position? If the original family consisted of a younger and an older child, say seven and ten years of age, and the step-child is a single child of eight, would that mean that the step-child loses his single-child characteristics and takes on the characteristics typical of a middle born? No, it doesn't. We establish the foundations of our identity between the ages of about three and six. A child will not suddenly lose characteristics that have been forming for years – they may enhance and embellish their identity, but are unlikely fundamentally to change it. So what's most likely to happen in this case is that the single and the eldest child will compete ferociously for the 'first born' position, and their respective first-born characteristics are likely to become more noticeable. At the same time, the youngest child may, if anything, become even *more* typically a last born.

When step-siblings are introduced into the home, older children are more likely to compete to uphold their previously established position in the family – perhaps even to build on it – in an attempt to sustain the level of attention they're used to receiving. Any child in a family whose birth-order position becomes less clear is likely to become more assertive, even aggressive, regardless of their age. On the other hand, when younger children are put into such situations, particularly if they're middle or last borns, they'll find it easier in some ways to adapt to their new birth-order position – that is, to take on additional qualities that are characteristic of their 'new' position in the family.

Overall, I think it's safe to say that the introduction of step-siblings is one of the most overlooked and yet critical factors that act on your character when you're growing up.

## The Return Home of an Older Sibling

The 'yo-yo' child is a fairly recent concept – the child who has grown up, left home and then returned because they couldn't find a job, has lost a job or, perhaps, couldn't find affordable housing. This is something that will affect everyone in the family – the individual who has been away, as well as their siblings.

When a first born leaves home, those who remain readjust their position in the family. I've said repeatedly that birth-order characteristics don't change radically after the age of about six or seven. What does happen, however, is that the expectations among the remaining children alter when an older sibling leaves the family home. The next child down becomes, in many senses, the eldest.

If the older child then returns, there's likely to be a clash – not so much of characters, but of assumed rights and privileges. In particular, the returning sibling and the 'acting eldest' are likely to compete and to fight more often and more openly. Alternatively, the 'acting eldest' whose new-found position has now been usurped, may withdraw and become sullen or angry.

The returning sibling is also likely to be suffering from lowered self-confidence due to the circumstances that have led to them coming home. They'll probably be feeling lost or without purpose and, because they are unlikely to have thought much about how their family might have changed in their absence, they may also be surprised to find that their parents treat their siblings differently now. This may add to any feelings of loneliness and worthlessness.

The outcome for everyone depends, crucially, on how parents deal with this situation. If you came back home to live for a time and your parents treated you as an adult rather than 'one of the kids' again, you and your siblings would have experienced less rivalry. So if they made it clear that they expected you to return to independent adult life – say, by setting a time limit for you to stay without paying rent – you probably will have felt more hopeful about re-establishing your independence. In short, although it appears a kindness when parents extend open arms unconditionally to a crest-fallen son or daughter, they unwittingly send a message that they're not sure when or how their child will recover and regain their sense of direction. This will only make the child feel less mature and less self-confident, and will confuse the other siblings.

These circumstances are unlikely to affect siblings' birth characteristics in the long term – only their moods and attitudes in the short term. However, if the situation is prolonged (say, for months rather than weeks) and there is no clear strategy to help the elder child move out again, it could cause everyone in the house to feel less optimistic about the future and perhaps more cynical generally. The younger ones, especially a less confident last born, may feel unenthusiastic about growing up and becoming independent themselves, lest they, too, 'fail' and are forced to return home.

## CASE STUDY: **George**

George was the second of four children. He had an older brother and two younger sisters. He was seventeen when he was referred to me for 'anger management', having recently become sullen and unpleasant at home, refusing to join in any family activities including mealtimes. He spent most of his time in his room playing computer games, and was missing quite a lot of school. Only a few months earlier, he'd started A levels enthusiastically and had seemed happy at home and at school.

George told me that he'd 'never been much good at anything'. He said that he'd always been overshadowed by his older brother Toby, who, it seemed, was brilliant at everything. Six years older than George, he'd attended university and then gone straight into an apprenticeship in the City where he 'did very well' and then he and his girlfriend had bought an expensive flat together in central London.

Once Toby left home, George had begun to flourish. He took up sports at school and joined the school rugby team. His grades improved, and he'd decided to take A levels, something his parents had previously not thought possible for him. In fact, he'd done very well in his first term.

However, by the end of George's first term at A level, Toby had moved back home. He'd lost his job and his flat, and he and his girlfriend had split up. The parents were extremely upset for Toby and pandered to his every whim at home. George had, predictably (to all but his parents, it seemed), withdrawn in every way.

Once George had expressed his hurt at being summarily replaced when Toby returned home, and once I'd commented that his distress wasn't unreasonable, he felt a great deal better. I then asked if we could invite his parents to join us, and he agreed. Initially, they seemed surprised at being included – they'd believed that the problem was all George's. However, they were willing to consider the situation from all points of view, and they soon saw how hurtful their focus on Toby had been for George. They also began to realise that by pandering to Toby, rather than encouraging him to help himself, they were curtailing his chances of rebuilding his life.

George's parents decided to talk to Toby. The three of them agreed that four months was a reasonable time limit for Toby to remain at home. It was, in fact, Toby who had suggested that this was the right amount of time for him to find some work and a new flat to rent. Meanwhile, they worked hard to give George the positive encouragement they'd begun to give him when he'd started his A levels.

George was soon back in school, and although the atmosphere at home was still difficult at times, he was already feeling much better, and his more optimistic and affable attitude had begun to resurface.

## The Introduction of an Infirm or Elderly Relative

There are a number of situations where someone who's not well or who's not coping either financially or in terms of self-care is brought into the family home to live. An increasingly common situation is for parents to assume the care of their own parents or grandparents. This is happening because, paradoxically, of improvements in health care: people are living longer, but are often more frail and dependent during much of that extended time.

The attitude of parents and the state of the person who moves in will determine most powerfully how the children in the family react to the new circumstances. If this happened when you were growing up and your parents assumed a positive attitude to the new set-up, it probably improved your sense of wellbeing and taught you some important lessons about caring for others.

Although all children may benefit in this situation, it's the first born who's most likely to become more nurturing and responsible, simply because they've always been expected to fill such a role.

There are cases where the newcomer doesn't want to move in – they may find it difficult to admit that they need more help, or perhaps they're confused. In these circumstances, although the children are still likely to help out and to become more aware of the needs of others, all of them (not just the first born) may also feel weighted down by the responsibility and/or jealous of the person who's taking so much of their parents' time and energy. In this situation, the last born, as the one who is used to being the most dependent member of the family, is likely to be more upset and to feel more 'displaced' than anyone else.

Furthermore, if family members feel chronically overtaxed by the demands that a newcomer puts on them, one or more of them – in particular, the first born – may then assume a 'victim' role. What that means is that whenever someone needs help, the person who's taken on a 'victim' role will wearily offer assistance, even when they've not been asked to do so.

---

### *Parenting tip: If you're caring for a relative in your home*

If you care for an infirm and/or frail person in your home, try never to ask too much of your children. In particular, be aware of the first born's tendency to nurture and take charge, so that they do not feel overly responsible. In addition, try as best you can not to appear overburdened yourself – so don't assume the 'victim' role (see above), although this may at times seem almost impossible. It's important to ensure that your children feel able to talk about the situation and that when they do, you respond honestly, but without appearing helpless.

---

## Birth-order Characteristics and Shake-ups in the Family: a Summary

Shake-ups in the family can evoke strong reactions in everyone involved, and this will be true of anything from moving house to something more profound such as parental separation. Stresses are especially likely if other people are introduced into the home. If any of these things happened when you were growing up, the effect it had on you depended crucially on how your parents handled the situation. If they felt overwhelmed and powerless in the face of the changed circumstances, or if they lost sight of their children's needs, then you – particularly if you are a first born – are likely to have adopted a fearful or anxious outlook on life. Everyone – but again, especially the first born – may also have lost some self-confidence, at least in the short term.

If, on the other hand, your parents assumed a positive attitude, treating the new situation as a problem to be solved and remembering to consider each child's point of view and best interests individually, then whatever happened probably strengthened and enhanced the character of all of the children in your family, regardless of their birth-order position.

## Chapter Eight

# Other Important Relationships

The people who influence you most when you're growing up are those in your immediate family. However, others may also play a role. In this chapter we'll be considering the roles that grandparents and other relatives, teachers and other authority figures, and friends and their families may have played in forming your character.

## Grandparents

It's often said that from a grandparent's point of view, the most delightful, inspiring and tender relationship they'll ever have is with their grandchildren. There's something overwhelmingly special about getting to know your own child's child, about seeing yourself and your child in this young person, glimpsing youthful enthusiasm once again and, at the same time, realising that this person is unique, unlike anyone you've ever encountered before. A grandchild grows up in a very different world from the one that their grandparent knew, so another advantage for grandparents of getting to know their grandchildren is that they learn about the current state of affairs through the eyes of someone who's growing up in that world.

You will have benefited enormously, regardless of your birth-order position, if you had grandparents you loved and who were involved in your life when you were growing up. A grandparent who was important in your life will have encouraged the development of patience and considered judgement. A grandparent also almost always adores their grandchild unreservedly – a vital resource for nurturing and maintaining self-confidence. This is why it's so important that there is a strong bond between children and their grandparents.

Too often these days, families are scattered far and wide, so in many cases it's difficult for grandparents to spend time with their grandchildren. At the other extreme, however, some parents may feel squeezed and pressured economically and they may, unintentionally, ask too much of their own parents in the way of childcare. In those cases, grandparents may feel that they're overburdened and that they're being taken advantage of. So although the relationship with their grandchildren will probably still be a positive one, it may not be as rich as it might have been without the stresses and strains imposed by feeling the obligation to care rather than choosing freely to do so.

## Other Relatives

Relationships with other relatives may also have affected your character. Many relatives today tend not to live near one another, so children do not always have an opportunity to form close and influential extended-family relationships. When it does occur, however, a child will benefit from having another person near by who loves them – someone who will be an additional role model and whose positive characteristics (hopefully) they may adopt.

All of these relationships can benefit everyone, regardless of their birth-order position, by adding to their sense of security and self-confidence. However, the extra love and attention will be especially welcome in larger families, and for those who may otherwise have been 'short-changed' when it came to receiving individual attention – middle borns, for example.

## *Abusive relationships*

It would be remiss to ignore the possibility that a relationship – whether with a relative or with anyone in the sections covered below – could have a very negative effect on someone's character. This is when abuse is involved – that is, where the more powerful individual uses the relationship solely to fulfil needs of their own and with total disregard to the other person's rights and needs, using physical, emotional or verbal abuse. When this happens, the effect is extremely powerful. It's likely to create in the abused a sense of helplessness and guilt, and a desperate need to be approved of and loved. Even much older children can be made to feel that an abusive relationship is their fault, and young children will inevitably feel that way (although sometimes it is only with hindsight that they are able to define the relationship as 'abusive').

An abusive relationship also leaves the abused more vulnerable than others to making poor choices when they grow up and start to form relationships themselves. Because they grow up with such a negative role model, then – unless they also had strong positive role models in their life, and unless they find someone they can trust to help them work through what happened – they're at risk of repeating the pattern of abuse, either as abusers themselves, or by again being abused.

A child's position in the family does not seem to be a consistent factor in these relationships, although birth-order characteristics may be affected by them.

## Teachers and Other Authority Figures

Perhaps there was a teacher in your life who influenced the way you think and behave? He or she might have introduced you to a subject that laid the groundwork for your current career; or perhaps that teacher simply encouraged you to love learning generally and to do well academically. A teacher may have had such a powerful impact on you that you not only adopted their love of learning, but decided to become a teacher yourself. Conversely, they could have caused you to dislike a subject – sometimes for the rest of your life – if they were particularly inept when teaching.

Other authority figures may also have exerted a similarly powerful influence on you. One of my patients was chronically ill as a child. She was so well cared for, particularly by one nurse who believed, in the face of all odds, that she'd recover, that once she did recover she chose to become a nurse herself.

You may also have had a friend whose parents influenced your character. This is particularly likely if for a time you weren't getting on with your own parents for some reason. A number of my patients have told me that they owe their optimistic outlook, determination or sense of humour, for example, to a friend's mother or father.

Of all the birth-order positions, those who are first borns tend to accept most readily what they are told by authority figures.

---

### *Flashbulb moments can affect groups too*

In addition to events that have a global impact or more personal flashbulb moments (see pages 105 and 130, respectively) incidents can also happen that will change the outlook of an entire community or ethnic group.

When I was in primary school, a child on the other side of our small town was kidnapped and murdered. The killer apparently did so without a motive and the community's reaction was immediate. Parents across our town stopped allowing their children to walk to school, and traffic jams built up every school day from that time onwards – even after the killer was arrested and jailed.

A number of other young children were killed when I was growing up – in road accidents, for example. However, people did not react to these events in the same way, in part because road accidents weren't as unexpected and shocking as a murder (although for the families who lost their loved ones, these would, no doubt, be flashbulb moments). I'm sure many children (I, for one) grew up to be much more fearful and less independent than they would have been had the kidnap and murder not have taken place. The ripples caused by this flashbulb event will therefore have strongly influenced and altered the birth-order characteristics of a large number of people.

## Friends

Finally, your friends have affected (and will continue to affect) your character. The influence that friends exert is particularly potent during adolescence. Just before puberty and in early adolescence in particular, we all re-examine and, to some extent, reconfigure our identity. We'll do this a number of times throughout our lives. However, the difference during adolescence is that we think about ourselves primarily in terms of the peer group to which we feel we belong.

I'm sure you've seen groups of young teenagers who dress alike, wear their hair in the same way, use the same verbal expressions and so on. This need to identify with a 'group' is a crucial step towards understanding ourselves. Each of us needs to decide the sort of person we want to become and the group to which we wish to belong, and this is one of the ways we do this.

According to the psychologist Erik Erikson, this exploration early on in adolescence is a necessary precursor to full maturity. It makes it possible for us to form and maintain truly intimate relationships later in life. In effect, what Erikson is saying is that until we know with whom we belong and then (later on) in what ways we're unique within that belonging, we cannot truly 'lose' ourselves to another in an intimate relationship.

It's no exaggeration to say that the longer we live, the more important our friends will become. Not only do they help us to enjoy life more, they also help us to understand ourselves better. Of all the birth-order positions, middle borns are, perhaps, most attuned to their peers, although spacing between siblings, gender and the size of the family will all also have some bearing on the relative influence of friends.

## Parenting tip: When you disapprove of your child's friends

If your child forms a friendship with someone you dislike or disapprove of, try not to show your feelings. The more you openly discourage or resist your child's desire to become friends with someone you don't like, the more powerful that individual's influence on her character will be.

→

Begin by asking yourself if this friend is someone you simply dislike, or whether they're actually having a deleterious effect on your child. If you simply don't like them, try to overcome your feelings, and don't discourage the friendship. If, on the other hand, the friendship is actually bad for your child in some way, try to steer them away from that individual without making it obvious that this is what you're doing. This is because the more your child senses your disapproval, the more fascinating the person will seem and the more your child will be drawn to and influenced by them.

## Friends and the single child

It's worth mentioning the critically important role that friends and young relatives played in your life if you were a single child. Because you had no sisters or brothers, the lessons you'd normally have learned by interacting with siblings – tolerance, sharing and compromising to name but a few – are learned instead with your friends and others. Parents of singles are wise, therefore, when they make every effort to provide their offspring with numerous opportunities to spend time with peers. Those singles grow up more tolerant, better equipped to compromise and generally more socially adept than singles whose parents don't make similar efforts.

## Birth-order Characteristics and Other Relationships: a Summary

In modern Western society, the emphasis on the nuclear family means that when we're young, we're currently more influenced by our parents and siblings than we are by anyone else. Other individuals can, however, also make an impact on the development of our character, particularly during adolescence. The extent of that influence will be determined by how much time we spend with those others, our age at the time we do so, and the reasons that drew us together.

# Chapter Nine

# Temperament vs Experience – the Nature/Nurture Question

Scientific research – in particular, our knowledge of the structure of our genes – is opening new possibilities for our understanding of personality. Advances in unravelling and understanding human DNA and breakthroughs in neuro-psychology mean that we're constantly learning more about how our thoughts, beliefs, feelings and behaviours are formed and maintained.

Fortunately, one of the most helpful aspects of our growing understanding of the human psyche is that psychologists and other scientists have abandoned the notion of 'either/or' when it comes to the formation of character and the nature/nurture question. Every aspect of what we are is the result of *both* nature and nurture. However, the *relative* contribution of each has become the topic of enormous interest.

There would not be enough space here to consider every aspect of human character and the relative contributions of nature and nurture to each of them – nor would it all be relevant. So for the purposes of this chapter I have chosen to focus on those characteristics that are most pertinent to birth order. They are:

- characteristics that appear to be highly genetic
- characteristics that appear to be primarily learned

- characteristics over which the relative contributions of nature and nurture are hotly debated.

## Characteristics That Appear to Be Highly Genetic

I'll begin by highlighting several of the most notable and widely studied aspects of character that appear to be primarily genetic – the ones that we're probably born with. These characteristics are extremely impervious to change and are, therefore, best accepted and used to advantage, rather than resisted or challenged. They are also the ones that are most likely to confuse you if you're trying to guess someone's birth-order position. That's because you won't be able to tell easily whether the behaviour you're observing is the result of someone's genetic predisposition or their birth-order position.

---

### *The interaction between innate or learned characteristics and birth-order position: a quick guide*

Those qualities that appear to be primarily genetic will 'come through' strongly in your makeup, regardless of your birth-order position. On the other hand, those qualities that appear to be primarily learned will develop only insofar as your birth-order characteristics encourage that development. Finally, those qualities that develop as a result of both nature and nurture will interact with your birth-order characteristics, making the latter more or less pronounced, depending on whether your place in the family encouraged such characteristics to develop in the first place.

## Introversion/extroversion

The degree to which you enjoy socialising, the amount of excitement and danger you find comfortable and the extent to which you rely on the environment to spur you on to meet deadlines and to complete projects is known as the introversion/extroversion dimension. This dimension was first developed by Hans Eysenck, a psychologist who claimed a person's tendency to more introverted or extroverted behaviour is determined by the activity in a part of the brain known as the reticular activating system (RAS). This part of the brain helps to control our level of arousal. Introverts, claimed Eysenck, have a more active RAS, so they're by nature already more stimulated (from within themselves) than are extroverts, who are under-aroused within themselves. Therefore extroverts seek out stimulation, whereas introverts tend to avoid it.

I'm sure you're familiar with this dimension, and that you know people who represent the extreme ends of it. Someone who's very extroverted craves excitement. They take chances and often act on impulse. They need deadlines to goad them into action. They generally have lots of friends and love to party and to socialise generally. An extreme introvert, on the other hand, prefers to avoid excitement. They tend to be reserved and thoughtful, unwilling to make quick decisions. They are more comfortable with only a few intimate friends and may seem to others to be rather quiet and distant.

If someone is quite an extrovert, particularly if they love to socialise and to be the centre of attention at parties, you might well conclude that they are a last born. In truth, however, anyone in any birth-order position may be an extrovert.

One of the many things we've discovered is that it's extremely difficult to make an extrovert behave and think like an introvert and vice versa. It's best, therefore, to accept the extent to which you're an extrovert or an introvert and to use it to advantage rather than to try to change it. For example, respecting how extroverted or introverted you are can help you find the job that will suit you best. Extroverts are likely to thrive in open-plan offices and to do well at work that calls for tight, non-negotiable deadlines, whereas introverts will be happier working alone or with only a few people, doing work that requires research and reflection before an answer is required.

## Impulsive/reflective

To some extent, this dimension has features in common with the extroversion/introversion dimension; perhaps one day we'll find that they're closely linked in the brain. Eysenck described extroverted individuals as impulsive and introverts as people who 'look before they leap' – who are, in other words, reflective.

The degree to which you're impulsive (that is, you rush into action before stopping to think and do many things 'on the spur of the moment') or reflective (you stop to think things through and to consider all possible courses of action before making a decision) is one of the most stable and enduring characteristics of personality. The psychologist Jerome Kagan found that even very young babies exhibit impulsive or reflective behaviour reliably, adding further weight to the idea that this is primarily a genetically based characteristic.

The extent to which you are either impulsive or reflective appears to be fairly insensitive to variables such as your birth-order position. So again, this dimension can be confusing when it comes to trying to guess someone's place in the family pecking order. You might conclude that an impulsive risk taker is probably a last born, when in truth anyone in any birth-order position can be impulsive or a risk taker. Similarly, you might guess that a reflective, rational individual is a single, whereas once again, anyone in any birth-order position can be reflective and rational.

The degree to which you are impulsive or reflective is another aspect of your character that's best worked with, rather than something you try to change about yourself. However, those of you who are extremely impulsive may wish to practise strategies such as counting to ten before reacting to someone, or writing down several courses of action before making a decision. Similarly, the extremely reflective among you may wish to set yourself a deadline by which you must make up your mind when a proposal is put to you. However, apart from these extremes, working with your natural tendency to react impulsively or by reflection is the best way forward.

## The autistic spectrum

There's been an increase in the number of people diagnosed as being 'on the autistic spectrum'. However, it is my belief that we're *all* somewhere on the 'autistic spectrum'. There are vast numbers of people who to some extent lack imagination, who become somewhat upset when their routines are varied or who may, in varying degrees, avoid socialising (introverts fall into the latter category, for example). This doesn't make these individuals 'autistic', however – it simply describes a dimension of character along which we all find ourselves. True autism and the related condition Asperger's Syndrome are more common than they once were, it's true, but they're still rare disorders.

In any individual, the amount of order and stability that feels comfortable, the degree to which they are able to be imaginative or creative and how much social interaction feels right for them are the characteristics that form the basis of the 'autistic spectrum'. This appears to be another dimension that doesn't change much as a person grows up. Whether Asperger's Syndrome and autism are aspects of the same disorder or whether they're two separate dimensions of the same problem remains to be determined. Either way, autistic characteristics appear to be resistant to change throughout an individual's lifetime. Simon Baron-Cohen is the leading researcher in the UK who's studying autism and the autistic dimension – for more information, see References, page 179.

Once again, these characteristics might mislead you when trying to guess someone's birth-order position. If someone shows a need for orderliness and takes a very rational approach to life, you could conclude that they are a single. In truth, however, anyone in any birth-order position can possess these characteristics.

For our purposes, again, it's best simply to accept an individual's position on this 'autistic spectrum' and not to consider it a problem (unless of course the behaviours are stopping the person from doing what they want to do). As with the extroversion/introversion and impulsive/reflective dimensions, it's best to work with 'autistic' tendencies rather than to fight against them.

All three of the character aspects we've looked at in this section are, as we've established, very robust – that is, they rarely change as we grow older. They're so strong, in fact, that they tend to override any of the characteristics an individual might also develop as a result of their position in the family.

## Characteristics That Appear to Be Primarily Learned

Here, we consider some aspects of human character that seem to be almost entirely learned. These are the ones that can be traced back in an individual's history to discover why and how an individual has come to behave, feel or think in that particular way. The development of these characteristics is, therefore, heavily influenced by your birth-order position and the way you were raised.

The good news about these characteristics is that if you want to change the way you express them, you'll almost certainly be able to do so. There are a number of characteristics (I've chosen four of them) that an individual can expect to express in the way they want to. True, they may need to seek some guidance and to put in the time and energy needed to make the required changes, but change is always possible.

Therefore, with regard to the characteristics in this section, you can expect to exhibit any of them. They develop, as do your birth-order characteristics, in response to the environment in which you grow up.

Of course, you are most likely to find yourself on the favourable end of any of these 'acquired' dimensions if you have parents who loved you unconditionally and who created an atmosphere that allowed you to develop optimally. But even if that didn't happen, you can still make changes in the direction you desire, whatever your birth-order position.

Here, then, are four characteristics that are almost entirely acquired, or learned through experience:

## Self-confidence

This is a trust in your own abilities and judgement. It's a quality that's learned best and most easily if you grew up with parents who loved you for who you were, rather than for what you achieved. Psychologists call this 'unconditional love' and it's the basis of a positive sense of self. You're also more likely to have grown up self-confident if your parents let you know that they valued your intelligence and that they trusted you to make wise decisions; equally, if when you didn't act so wisely, rather than scolding or criticising you, they helped you to learn from your mistakes.

If no one cared for you in this manner when you were young, you can still achieve a high level of self-confidence by learning to praise and love yourself. It's far more difficult to do this as an adult than if it was shown to you as a child, but it can still be done. Seeking help from a skilled therapist is the most direct way to learn how to become self-confident, but being loved unconditionally by another individual can sometimes be enough – even if this only really happens for the first time as an adult.

## Ambition

Some people confuse impulsivity with ambition. Impulsivity means acting quickly, seizing the moment, but without a particular plan in mind. An ambitious person, on the other hand, decides what it is that they want to achieve and then seizes every opportunity to realise their goal.

Ambition is, once again, most likely to have been learned when you were a child. If your parents expected you to be a high achiever, and if they themselves set lofty goals and worked hard to reach them, the chances are that you will have become an ambitious person. None the less, if you did not have such an upbringing, it's still possible to learn how to set high, but achievable, standards for yourself by choosing role models who've done the sorts of things you hope to do, by learning how they went about it, then by adapting their strategies to your own circumstances.

Beware, however, of assuming that setting high ambitions goes hand in hand with being happy. Ambitions have a bad habit of simply breeding further ambitions, rather than bestowing satisfaction (or at least any sort of long-term satisfaction). The secret to being both ambitious and happy is to set ambitious goals, but to enjoy the process of realising them, rather than expecting to revel in the attainment itself. If an individual remains rooted in and aware of what they're doing in the present, then for them, ambition is likely to be an enjoyable spur to activity.

There is a relationship between ambition and birth-order characteristics: first borns are most likely to be described as ambitious. However, because they often set themselves high standards and lofty goals merely for the purpose of gaining praise and recognition from parents or other authority figures, their ambition seldom brings them happiness.

## Honesty

All children go through a stage when they tell lies. It's part of language development and, to that extent, it's an innate quality. So when a child starts telling lies, it simply means that they've come to understand that they can use language to deny what's actually happening or has happened.

However, although the ability to lie is universal and a sign of normal cognitive development, whether or not someone chooses to use it habitually is a decision based on learning. If your parents taught you, both by example and by patient explanation, the benefits and the importance of telling the truth, you'll almost certainly grow up valuing honesty and you won't deliberately tell lies. Those who punish their children for lying, but offer no alternative and better way of behaving or any explanation about why it's wrong to lie (and in particular those parents who themselves lie or cheat and then show delight when they get away with such behaviour) raise children who are also likely to lie and cheat to get what they want.

Whether or not you're honest or dishonest depends on the values you learned at home when you were young;

it's not associated in any particular way with birth-order position.

## Skills – the ability to communicate, socialise and organise yourself well

If someone is a competent communicator and socialiser, it won't help you to predict their birth-order position. None the less, there is an interaction between the acquisition of these skills and birth-order position.

First borns and singles will be more interested in developing good communication skills and singles will be particularly interested in learning how to be organised. On the other hand, last borns and middle borns will be keener to develop good social skills.

People often say that someone is 'lucky' or 'clever' if they're well organised, if they're good at meeting new people or if they express themselves well – as if this is something they've come by naturally. No one, however, is born with these characteristics. These are skills that are learned, both by observing others and also by practising the appropriate behaviours.

Genetics play a part in skills development by making it relatively easier or more difficult to learn various skills. For example, it's known that at birth a female's left brain hemisphere is relatively larger than the right hemisphere compared to males. Because language is located largely in the left hemisphere, this information has helped scientists understand that brain structure is one of the main reasons why girls seem to outpace boys when they're first learning to speak.

To take another example, some people (extroverts) are keener to meet new people and to socialise than are others (introverts). Therefore, it's likely to be easier for extroverts to acquire good 'party' skills than it will be for introverts, because they'll enjoy the learning. But these tendencies merely set the scene. The content – the actual behaviours and strategies – needed for competency in any skill is learned.

Once again, it's easiest to learn skilled behaviours if they are modelled by parents and children are rewarded for behaving similarly when they are growing up. None the less, as with self-confidence, honesty and ambition, any of these qualities can be learned later in life. Finding a role model to copy, following the suggestions in self-help books, and/or attending courses are all good ways to acquire and enhance any of these skills.

## Characteristics Over Which the Relative Contributions of Nature and Nurture are Hotly Debated

Here, we examine those characteristics that continue to be highly controversial with regard to the relative contributions of nature and nurture.

### Intelligence

If by 'intelligence' we mean IQ scores, then we're talking about something that's definitely more of an acquired characteristic than a genetic one. However, the concept of intelligence has now been re-examined and, thankfully, elaborated and refined. Most scientists today no longer consider intelligence to be a single entity, defined by one or two 'scores', but rather a number of different capacities ranging from linguistic intelligence to bodily awareness to social intelligence – and each of these develops from both genetic and learned bases. The best discussion I know on this subject, even though it's now somewhat dated, is Howard Gardner's book *Frames of Mind* (see References, page 179).

How intelligent someone appears to be may help you to predict their birth-order position – but only if you define intelligence *merely* in terms of IQ. That is, first borns and singles are most likely to work hard to achieve high IQ scores; in other words, to learn how to succeed in school and in particular to communicate well verbally. On the other hand, if you define intelligence as Howard Gardner does – that is, as a quality that can express itself in a number of different ways, whether through music, art, mathematics or athletics, for example – it is unlikely to help you in predicting someone's birth-order position.

## Optimism/pessimism

Until fairly recently, most people assumed that your general outlook – that is, how optimistically or pessimistically you view life – is something you learn entirely as a result of your upbringing and experience. However, early in 2009, researchers from the University of Essex claimed to have found that individuals with a specific genetic variation tend to seek out positive images and to avoid negative ones. Of course, it's very early days, but what this study suggests is that there may be a genetic contribution to one's outlook on life, and that this could play a substantial role in determining our view of the world.

As far as birth order is concerned, there's no reliable correlation between this dimension and birth-order characteristics. The optimistic/pessimistic dimension is more closely related to the way you were parented than it is to your position in the family.

## Creativity

There's a long-held belief that some individuals are born with talent or with a particular creative ability, while others simply are not; and furthermore, that if you aren't born with a particular ability you'll never be considered gifted or a genius. It's surprising that this view has any acceptance at all given the fact that 'geniuses' and those with 'real talent' always work incredibly hard at their 'gift'.

The truth is that with creativity, as with intelligence and optimism, the relative contributions of nature and nurture have only just begun to be untangled and, in actual fact, whatever innate talent you may have, experience will also play a role in its expression.

There appears to be a strong relationship between creativity and birth order. According to psychological research carried out by Frank Sulloway, a disproportionate number of creative, innovative individuals are last borns. I suspect there are two reasons for this. Firstly, last borns are generally less pressured by their parents to develop in a particular way, so they're freer to discover their own particular talents and gifts. Secondly, in order to distinguish themselves from their older siblings, last borns usually have to find a less conventional (and therefore, more often creative or groundbreaking) way of attracting attention.

## Birth-order Characteristics and the Nature/Nurture Issue: a Summary

My own view about the characteristics I've presented in this chapter is that even those qualities that are weighted heavily towards 'nature' can be changed to some degree, while those that are weighted towards 'nurture' will contain at least some innate basis. All our characteristics, whether they're typical of a particular birth-order position or not, are a fundamental part of each of us, yet are also open to modification.

That's why it's so important to remember that when you're trying to understand yourself or other people better, although birth-order characteristics may describe someone to a large extent, they can't be a complete guide to anyone's character. You'll find that you can understand yourself and others better if you look at the whole picture.

# A Last Word

Anyone who's read my other books will know that *The Prophet* is my favourite book. When it comes to understanding the uniqueness and complexity of the human character, I don't think anyone knows more than Kahlil Gibran.

When a man asks Gibran's Prophet to explain how we can truly know ourselves, the Prophet warns him of the enormity of the task by telling him that 'self is a sea boundless and measureless'. When we try to understand ourselves, or our 'soul', as the Prophet refers to it, he cautions us thus:

> Say not, 'I have found the truth,' but rather, 'I have
>     found a truth.'
> Say not, 'I found the path of the soul.' Say rather,
>     'I have met the soul walking upon my path.'
> For the soul walks upon all paths.
> The soul walks not upon a line, neither does it grow
>     like a reed.
> The soul unfolds itself, like a lotus of countless
>     petals.
>
> The Prophet, Kahlil Gibran, 1923

# References

Ansbacher, H. L. and Ansbacher, R. R., *The Individual Psychology of Alfred Adler*, George Allen and Unwin, 1958.
(Alfred Adler is generally considered to be the first psychologist to have ascribed importance to birth order. His description of each birth-order position is given on pages 372–83.)

Baron-Cohen, Simon and Bolton, Patrick, *Autism: The Facts*, Oxford University Press, 1993.
(This book explains what causes autism – including possible biological and physiological causes – and how the condition is recognised and diagnosed.)

Blair, Linda, *The Happy Child: Everything You Need to Know to Raise Enthusiastic, Confident Children*, Piatkus, 2009.
(In particular, you might find the discussions on autism and on Diana Baumrind's parenting styles helpful.)

Dahl, Roald, *The Witches*, Puffin Books, 1983.
(This book includes a vivid description of a 'flashbulb moment', when the narrator learns that his parents have been killed in a car crash.)

Erikson, Erik H., 'Identity and the Lifecycle', Monograph, *Psychological Issues*, vol. I, no. 1, International Universities Press, 1959.

(This is the best discussion I know about how we form our identity.)

Forrest, A. D., Affleck, J. W. and Zealley, A. K. (eds), *Companion to Psychiatric Studies, Second Edition,* Churchill Livingstone, 1978.
(The editors summarise Eysenck's theory of personality on pages 187–8, discussing in particular the introversion/extroversion dimension.)

Fox, E., Ridgewell, A. and Ashwin, C., 'Looking on the Bright Side: Biased Attention and the Human Serotonin Transporter Gene', *Proceeding of the Royal Society B,* published online before print on 25 February 2009.
(This is the University of Essex study about the inheritability of optimism.)

Gardner, Howard, *Developmental Psychology: An Introduction,* Little, Brown and Co., 1978.
(This, in my opinion, is the finest book on child development in print.)

Gardner, Howard, *Frames of Mind: The Theory of Multiple Intelligences,* Paladin Books, 1987.
(Gardner describes six types of human intelligence, how they come about and how to recognise them.)

Gladwell, Malcolm, *Outliers: The Story of Success,* Penguin Books, 2008.
(Gladwell tells a story brilliantly. He's talking in this book about why some people are successful and others not. In particular, he talks about the need for massive effort and practice to be considered a 'genius' in Chapter 2.)

Grose, Michael, *Why First Borns Rule the World and Last Borns Want to Change It,* Random House Australia, 2003.
(In my opinion this is a bit light and jokey, but none the less worth reading.)

Herrnstein, Richard J. and Murray, Charles, *The Bell Curve: Intelligence and Class Structure in American Life,* Free Press, 1994.
(This book bravely discusses the heritability of IQ. In particular, take a look at Chapters 13 and 14 about racial differences in IQ.)

Kagan, J. and Moss, H., *Birth to Maturity: A Study in Psychological Development,* John Wiley, 1962.
(This is one of the best longitudinal studies in psychology, following children in the small town of Fels, Ohio, from birth to seventeen years. Kagan and Moss discuss the impulsive/reflective dimension.)

Konig, Karl, *Brothers and Sisters: The Order of Birth in the Family,* Floris Books (Steiner Publications, Inc.), 2004.
(This is somewhat dated and contains what I consider to be some odd ideas about birth order, but the discussion about how hard it is to learn much from birth-order position alone is good.)

Moore, Anna, 'First Person', the *Guardian* ('Family' section), 29 November 2008.
(A nice account of what it feels like as a middle child of three daughters.)

Pinker, Steven, 'Why Nature and Nurture Won't Go Away', *Daedelus,* vol. 33, no. 4, fall 2004.
(This is quite scholarly, but beautifully written. Pinker talks about how to define and value the contributions of both 'nature' and 'nurture' in human development.)

Richardson, Ronald and Richardson, Lois, *Birth Order and You,* Self-Counsel Press, 2000.
(This is easy to read, although I think there are too many sub-categories for birth position; there are lots of case histories.)

Roberts, Yvonne, *Grit: The Skills for Success – How They are Grown,* The Young Foundation, 2009.
(This is an absolute goldmine of up-to-date studies and references considering why some kids grow up to be happy and successful while others don't – and, of course, that means there's a discussion of the nature/nurture debate. It's beautifully written.)

Sulloway, Frank J., *Born to Rebel: Birth Order, Family Dynamics, and Creative Lives,* Little, Brown and Co., 1996.
(This is fairly scholarly, but it contains an incredibly rich and interesting argument, with many examples of historical characters and of how birth order and attitudes are linked. In particular, Sulloway argues that creative people and those who make scientific breakthroughs are almost always last borns.)

Sulloway, Frank and Zweigenhaft, Richard, 'Birth Order and Risk Taking in Athletics: A Meta-Analysis and Study of Major League Baseball', *Personality and Social Psychology Review*, 30 April 2010; Alan Schwarz, 'From Big Leagues, Hints at Sibling Behavior', *New York Times*, Science section, D1 24 May 2010.
(This paper is illustrative of Sulloway's usual approach – thorough, sound and comprehensive. At the same time, because he is talking about baseball – one of America's greatest passions – it has a more light-hearted feel to it than does his book.)

Winner, Ellen, *Gifted Children,* Basic Books, 1996.
(In this elegant book, Winner describes what it means to be 'gifted'. In particular, have a look at her 'Nine Myths about Giftedness' – Chapter 1.)

# Index